M000105581

WHAT'S YOUR

Mom Type?

WHAT'S YOUR

Mom Type?

DISCOVERING
GOD'S DESIGN
FOR YOU

DALE WILSHER

What's Your Mom Type? Discovering God's Design for You
Published by Morgan Reid Press
Erie, CO

Copyright ©2019 Dale Wilsher. All rights reserved.

No part of this book may be reproduced in any form or by any mechanical means, including information storage and retrieval systems without permission in writing from the publisher/author, except by a reviewer who may quote passages in a review.

All images, logos, quotes, and trademarks included in this book are subject to use according to trademark and copyright laws of the United States of America.

ISBN: 978-0-578-42949-6

RELIGION / Christian Living / Parenting

Cover by Victoria Wolf

Unless otherwise noted, all scripture verses are taken from the THE HOLY BIBLE, NEW INTERNATIONAL VERSION®, NIV® Copyright © 1973, 1978, 1984, 2011 by Biblica, Inc.® Used by permission. All rights reserved worldwide.

Scripture taken from The Message. Copyright © 1993, 1994, 1995, 1996, 2000, 2001, 2002. Used by permission of NavPress Publishing Group.

Holy Bible, New Living Translation, copyright © 1996, 2004, 2015 by Tyndale House Foundation. Used by permission of Tyndale House Publishers, Inc., Carol Stream, Illinois 60188. All rights reserved.

Scripture taken from the New Century Version®. Copyright © 2005 by Thomas Nelson. Used by permission. All rights reserved.

QUANTITY PURCHASES: Schools, companies, professional groups, clubs, and other organizations may qualify for special terms when ordering quantities of this title. For information, email hello@yourauthenticpersonality.com.

All rights reserved by Dale Wilsher and Morgan Reid Press
This book is printed in the United States of America.

This book is dedicated to my girls,
Savannah, Casey, Caroline, and Ansley,
whose precious lives have helped me reclaim my authentic self.

Some characters mentioned in this book are composites of real people. Names and identifying details have been changed to protect the privacy of individuals.

TABLE OF CONTENTS

My Promise to You

Dear Mom,

The book you hold in your hands is one solution to the mystery of you.

Granted, it won't cover everything about you—you're simply too complex for that—but it will provide insight into your innate design and your authentic personality: your best self the way God intended you to be.

It's unique in that this message is written by a mom, for moms, with mom examples. Sure, you can find books about personality types written by and for academics, business leaders, or even the masses. Most of that material is thick with psychological terms and filled with examples from the workplace. But mothers—women with the most significant role in our society who are raising and influencing the next generation—have gotten *nada*.

Until now.

Think of me as your translator. As a certified trainer for the DISC personality assessment, and as a researcher of personality-based material for the past twenty years, I've taken all the literature, condensed it, and translated it into mom language, with mom labels, and real-life mom examples. I've kept the chapters short and practical, addressing your lack of time as one of your top concerns.

Here is what you can hope to discover about yourself:

- Unlock the mystery of who you are and how God designed you.
- Understand your signature strengths and how they can positively impact your family.
- Accept your type-specific limitations and allow God to grow you in your areas of weakness.
- Live authentically, not hiding who you are, but displaying God's reflection to your family, friends, and neighbors.
- Thrive in your originality in a digital world that seeks to mold you into someone you were never intended to be.
- Clarify your mom mission so you can parent according to God's direction and design.
- Learn your unique leadership style as a mom so you can use your strengths to bless your children.

I can't wait for you to experience the freedom and empowerment that come when you understand your God-given personality and the intention for which He created you.

With love and hope,
Dale

CHAPTER 1

Why Is It So Hard to Know Yourself?

There's someone I want you to meet.

You.

Before you start checking yourself in the mirror, I'm not talking about the "got-it-all-together" you who hides your insecurities, failures, and that secret stash of junk food in your bathroom drawer.

I'm not talking about the chameleon you who instinctively changes to match the thoughts, feelings, and expectations of those around you.

And I'm certainly not talking about the depleted you who's sleep-deprived and brain-dead, constantly trying to catch up and desperate to make it through one more day.

But the real you.

The authentic you.

Your purest and best self.

I want you to come face-to-face with the you that God imagined when He knit you together in your mother's womb and wove particular skills, desires, and purposes into your very DNA. The naked, unashamed you in all your wonder and beauty that existed before you started layering on false images designed to impress, to fit in, or merely to survive.

In unguarded moments—when you race your son to the end of the block in a burst of wild energy, or you fall headlong into the eyes of your daughter as she studies you with undefiled adoration—you glimpse the way God sees your soul and the beauty and potential of your design. You think: *Part of me is buried—somehow unknown—as if I'm not seeing all of who I am,* but before you can explore the idea, life crashes in. Your toddler has a meltdown. The dog pees on the carpet. The principal calls. You simply don't have the time or energy—or maybe the permission—to pursue what lies beneath.

I know this is true because, for many years, I lived with an undiscovered self. I couldn't tell you about my authentic personality to save my life.

It started when, as a child, I was told that I was bossy and waaaay too loud. My young mind translated this to mean that my personality was flawed and must be changed. I wanted to be a good girl, so I buried the "bigger" parts of me and tried to keep my mouth shut. In an effort to be more pleasing to those around me, I started the journey away from my true self.

In college, I took my first personality test. The results affirmed what people had said about me in my youth: that I was direct, determined, and dominant. *No, no, please no.* Those were not the qualities with which I wanted to be associated. I wanted to be gentle and sweet, like the girls who got dates. I closed my eyes to who I was and tried to become something I was not, further burying the real me.

With every passing year, I became more removed from my

authentic self. In avoiding the bad, I had avoided the good, too. I didn't know my strengths. I didn't understand my worth. And I was completely unaware that God had purpose in my design. It had all gotten lost in the shuffle of life.

By the time I'd given birth to four girls, I felt completely diminished about who I was as I poured what was left of me into them.

Other mothers do this as well.

Brooke, a stay-at-home mom of two, lost her own identity somewhere between the aisles of Babies "R" Us and the bleachers at soccer practice. She immersed herself in the lives of her children to the point that she no longer knew where they ended and her true self began.

Hannah, a part-time nurse and mom of three, never really knew who she was from the beginning. She learned early on that the way to keep the peace with the strong personalities in her life was to agree with them. She attended the college her parents recommended, majored in the degree her advisor suggested, and married her very first boyfriend. She didn't rock the boat, and her life just kind of drifted into place. But all that "going with the flow" never taught her who she was or how to live with intention and purpose.

Kathryn, a business owner and stepmom of two, is probably the most polite person I've ever met. She genuinely cares about and has compassion for others. But her constant focus on their opinions (always wondering, *What will people think?)* has made her deaf and dumb to what she feels, to who she is, or how God has designed her.

As a speaker at women's retreats and MOPS (Mothers of Preschoolers) groups, my mission is to help moms understand their authentic personalities because it's so difficult to do. Buried under loads of laundry, dirty dishes, and the stress of meeting everyone else's needs, a mother's true self and her greatest assets are in desperate need of a search and rescue.

Why don't moms know their true selves?

Here are five of the most common reasons they give. As you read, consider whether any of these obstacles are keeping you from knowing your authentic self.

Five Obstacles in Your Way

1. I don't have time. Admittedly, it takes focused "you" time to learn about your true self, and yet time is probably the exact thing you find in short supply.

The only alone time you get is when you fill your gas tank.

"Me time" is a glimpse of yourself in the rearview mirror.

Downtime—what's that?

I get it. Motherhood isn't exactly known as the season of self-reflection. When your schedule is packed as tight as sardines, with school obligations, kid activities, and work deadlines, it's extremely difficult to stretch out with a good book and get to know yourself.

So I'm going to make this quick.

It's critical that you understand the best you have to offer your children, so you can be confident in your role and effective as their leader. There's no time to lose.

And I promise you, it will take less time than you imagine.

2. Social media messages confuse me about who I am, or who I should be. You scroll through Facebook and see CrossFit mom who posts selfies with her beautiful baby and beautiful abdominals—two things you didn't think could go together. Then there's a picture of FreeRange mom who posts about the scramlette she just whipped up with eggs from her very own chickens. Proudmama boasts about her son's 4.5 GPA and his selection for leadership camp. Playdate mom posts a live video of herself at the park with her twenty closest friends and all of their little ones. A mom on Pinterest shows you how easy it is to make your own curtains, aerate your yard, and grout your shower—all before lunch.

With each additional post, you feel less confident about how you are managing your household.

It's not just the updates on a few moms, but hundreds or thousands, depending on the size of your friend list and the number of pages you like.

Face it. Your news feed is stacked against you. Every blog, ad, and photo speaks of who you should be and tempts you to judge yourself as inadequate. These synthetic images shame your authentic self. No wonder you're confused, depressed, and feeling inadequate.

3. It's hard to be authentic in a world that promotes fake. Fake is everywhere. You turn on the TV and get fake storylines. You go to the grocery store and see faux food. You stop at Target and hope to find a knockoff brand that looks just as good as the original designer.

Fake nails, false eyelashes, and beefed-up breasts have become the new norm.

You see fake moms who manufacture phony realities. The mom who *never* struggles, *never* yells (that's a good one), *never* doubts, and *always* wears a smile. Her children are perfect. Her marriage is perfect. Oh yeah, she forgot to mention that it takes serious pharmaceutical support to try to pull this off.

The artificial life seduces you with lies about who you should be and what you could be, if you only tried a little harder. You don't want to be fake, but the fakeness around you sucks you in and, even though you resist, you sometimes pretend to be something you're not, because if you don't, the real you will be judged, pitied, or rejected altogether.

4. Focusing on me feels selfish. Caregivers (aka good mothers) give loads of love and care to others. It's what we do. We give in the morning when we make breakfast for the family and pack lunches for the day. We give in the afternoon when we shop for groceries, clean the toilets, or pay the bills. We give in the evenings when we make yet another meal and help with homework. We give from sunup to sundown, making sure everyone has exactly what they need. But after a while, all this giving can lead us to believe that it's selfish to receive. It just feels wrong, like we're stealing time and energy from our families, which is why we grapple with self-care and asking for help.

And then there's our faith. We're taught as Christians that we're to be *selfless, not selfish*. We're to lay down our lives for others rather than look out for number one. Granted, this is a valid teaching in the Bible, but we've mistakenly made this an either/or proposition. Either you sacrifice yourself *or* you're selfish, with little room for anything in between. It's true, God doesn't want you to be driven by selfish ambition (Philippians 2:3). We are not to think too highly of ourselves (Romans 12:3). But that doesn't mean He wants us to ignore ourselves or live in the dark about the gifts and strengths He's entrusted to us.

It's an issue of stewardship. If you are to truly give of yourself, with intention, you need to know what exactly you have to give.

5. It's hard to be my authentic self when I feel I need to be well-rounded. Your dentist wants you to floss. Your HOA wants you to paint your house. Your husband wants a hot dinner. Your kids want your undivided attention. Your dog wants you to take him for a walk. Your mother wants you to call her. Everyone wants a piece of you and there's not enough to go around.

Moms are pressured every day by the expectations of others. I surveyed more than 600 women, most of them moms, and asked them to rate the degree to which they feel that type of pressure. The question was stated like this: "On a scale of one to ten with one being not much and ten being very much, how much do the expectations of others affect you?" Sixty-seven percent of women said seven or higher with over half of that number reporting nine or above. That's a lot of pressure.

How's a mom supposed to know herself, much less *be* herself, when a multitude of voices from her church, her employer, her family, and her friends, are all pointing her in the "right" direction and telling her how and where to march?

E.E. Cummings said, "To be nobody-but-yourself—in a world which is doing its best, night and day, to make you everybody else—means to fight the hardest battle which any human being can fight; and never stop fighting."[1]

But there is hope.

You have an authentic personality.

You can discover it.

It doesn't have to take a lot of time.

Understanding your true self will absolutely make you a better mom, wife, and person.

I promise this is so, because I've witnessed this in the lives of the moms I coach and in my own life.

Uncover Your Authentic Personality

The first time I was introduced to my authentic self was when I was a mom of young children. At that time, I was disenchanted with myself because I'd never heard my personality type described in favorable terms. But my friend Shannon, who led our couple's study one week, introduced us to four temperaments of personality. She listed more than twenty positive character traits that described me and my type (please see www.yourauthenticpersonality.com/slice-sheets for lists for each type). She was complimentary, affirming, and encouraging. She told me that God had chosen this type for me and that it was a blessing and not a curse. As she spoke, something in me started to come to life.

Her explanation of my personality brought me out of hiding and called up the courage I needed to start living authentically, stewarding my God-given strengths with purpose and confidence. It made me a much better reflection of God and a much better mom.

At age forty-seven, shockingly, I found myself divorced after twenty-four years of marriage. I was suddenly thrust into caring for four teenage daughters literally by myself, and going back to work after years of staying at home with my kids. I realize now that I wouldn't have been able to survive those tumultuous times without my unique personality frame. Never had I been so thankful for the grit, organization, and independence infused into my being by a loving Father who knew I would one day need these qualities. Like a suitcase that had already been packed for me, God loaded me up for my journey before I was even born.

And I have news for you. He's done the same for you.

I share this message with my clients on a daily basis. As a certified life coach, I help them discover their authentic selves and all the potential that God has woven into their designs. I've witnessed the transformational power of personality awareness as they come to see themselves as God sees them. I call it divine self-awareness.

How This Will Work

In the next chapter, you'll learn about God's plan for your personality and what it means to be made in His image. It's vital that you understand how intricately God wove your personality together and infused it with a uniqueness that delights Him. To know your true self, you must also know God, because knowing self and knowing God are interdependent.

In Chapter 3, you'll get your first glimpse at the four Authentic Mom Types and be able to take the Authentic Mom Personality Test. This chapter provides additional questions to help you clarify your true type, as well as information about the tendencies that can skew your results. Once you've worked your way through all that, you'll be ready to know more.

Each of the even-numbered chapters (4, 6, 8, and 10), describes one Authentic Mom Type in detail: her strengths, weaknesses, leadership qualities, self-care needs, and mom triggers. These five elements will repeat for each type, but the introduction, information, and style of writing are unique to each type.

Each of the odd-numbered chapters (5, 7, 9, and 11), explains the ways you are like God, the predominant lie your type believes, and the life-changing truth that will set you free. Some of the language, especially in reference to the lies, is consistent in all four chapters because every mom, regardless of type, will face this problem. But the journey to truth is different for each Authentic Mom Type. You won't want to miss the spiritual discipline that will help you go deeper with God and discover His design for you.

Chapter 12 shows each mom how to stay authentic by tapping into the uniqueness of those around her. This chapter will free you to be who and how God made you, inspire you to live out your authenticity in community, and tap into the strengths of those around you.

I encourage you to read *every* chapter (not just the type in which you score highest on the test) for three important reasons. First, it helps to see the "real you" spelled out in greater detail. You'll discover new things about yourself that will open the door to new possibilities. Second, most moms have a major *and* a minor Authentic Mom Type. You'll find out if you have more than one in your test results. Finally, understanding all four types will give you insight about the personalities of the people around you—why they act as they do and what motivates them—especially those in your family.

Ralph Waldo Emerson said, "Our chief want is someone who will inspire us to be what we know we could be."[2] I hope and pray that, through the words on these pages, and through the power of the Holy Spirit, you may be inspired to know your true self.

To know your true self, you must begin with God, because He had a purpose in mind when He created you as He did.

Are you ready to see what God envisioned for your life before it even began?

In the next chapter, you'll discover your slice of God's image.

CHAPTER 2

What's Your Slice?

A mom walked past her infant son's nursery and was surprised to hear a voice coming from inside his room. Thinking he was a little young to be forming words, she quickly opened his door to check it out. Beside his crib stood Annie, her four-year-old daughter. The mom listened quietly, then smiled, when she heard Annie's urgent plea. "Quick, Samuel," she whispered. "Tell me where you came from. I'm beginning to forget."

Where do we come from? It's a question each of us asked at some point in our childhoods, but we probably didn't seek the answer from our baby brothers. They're not exactly known to deliver sage advice.

Instead, we asked the question of our parents.

Years ago, moms and dads told their children that they came from the stork. Can you believe that actually worked? It's a bird, for crying out loud. But as parents today, we're far more sophisticated. We respond with phrases like, "It's complicated" or "That's a great question," then pause just long enough for them to forget what we were talking about. Or we give the age-appropriate technical explanation and hope it goes right over their heads. We might even tell our children that they came from Mom and Dad's love.

Sweet, but still confusing.

What's the right answer then?

I believe it's this: We come from God. This is crucial to keep in mind as you discover your authentic personality. Because if you don't know where you're from, it's hard to know who you are.

The Image of God

After five successful days creating everything from the sun and the stars to the fish in the sea, the Father, Son, and Holy Spirit huddled up together and said, "Let us make mankind in our image, in our likeness" (Genesis 1:26).

If you read the entire first chapter of the Bible, you can feel the anticipation build. Every single day that God made something new, He proclaimed it as "good." But what He was about to create next would be "so good, so *very* good!" (Genesis 1:31 MSG, italics mine). This would be the grand finale of creation. It had to be exciting. It needed to be extraordinary. Better than anything that had come before. This would be the greatest work ever to come out of the heart and the mind of God. As the French say, God's pièce de résistance.

So what did God create?

Man and woman.

Humankind.

You.

The fact that you are God's masterpiece is significant.

It means that you're more beautiful than a sunset
(even *with* stretch marks on your belly and spit-up in your hair),
more awe-inspiring than a supernova
(even *without* shaved legs or a decent night's sleep),
and more remarkable than any living creature ever to walk the earth. All because you were made in His image.

Let that sink in.

For many years, I didn't get this concept. I didn't see myself through the lens of God and had no idea that I was "fearfully and wonderfully made" (Psalm 139:14).

When I was a young girl, I noticed that my younger brother looked exactly like my dad. They had the same build, the same smile, and the same crew cut. Once a month on Saturday morning, because apparently there was nothing better for me to do, I'd go with them to the barbershop to watch them surrender what was left of their hair. It was relatively quick and painless, so I'd sit quietly and watch. When the deed was done, the barbers removed the capes and brushed away all the little pieces of hair from their necks, and then said to my dad while looking at my brother, "He's the spitting image of you." And they were right. Nearly bald people always look alike. Then they'd turn to the waiting area, look at me and ask, "Who does she look like?" We'd all shrug our shoulders and smile politely because we had no answer. I didn't appear to be the spitting image of anyone.

What I've learned in the years since is that, while I may not look like anyone in my family, I am the spitting image of God, and so are you. We look like Him. We reflect something of Him. We bear the family resemblance.

Caroline Leaf, in her book, *The Perfect You*, says it this way:

You are a specific part of His reflection, the missing piece that brings a unique perspective and hope to the world. When you are not you, we all miss out on knowing God better, because you reflect His image in a unique and beautiful way.[3]

You come from God. He is your source; you are His reflection.

The question is, what exactly do we reflect that looks like God? Are we to be *omniscient* like God, knowing all things and reading everyone's mind? Are we to be *omnipresent* like God, driving the carpool for one child, while watching dance practice for another, and making dinner at the same time? Are we to be *omnipotent* like God, reigning over all the affairs of our families and exerting our authority so that our will be done?

No, of course not. Your job description isn't quite that big.

Your Slice of God's Image

My family is from Georgia, so my favorite pie is pecan, the nut of the south. Every year at Thanksgiving, we make at least two pies. The sugary aroma of caramel and toasted pecans fills the entire kitchen. My mouth waters just thinking about it. There's nothing quite like that first bite when the warm, soft filling and buttery crust melt in my mouth. If I didn't have a family who also loved pecan pie, I'd probably eat the whole thing by myself! But, because I need to share, I get a slice.

That slice is my portion.

Think of God as the whole pie. He is the sum total of every virtue, such as wisdom, justice, grace, and mercy. By making us in His image, He shares those with us, but we don't get them all—we get a slice.

God's comprehensive nature is simply too vast to be reflected in any one person, so God created different types of people, different types of moms, and different types of slices to reflect His many features. You and I get a slice of God's image. As the Psalmist said, "LORD, you have assigned me my portion and my cup" (Psalm 16:5).

Your distinct personality, the one crafted by God, is your slice of His image.

$$\frac{My\ Slice}{God's\ Image} = Authentic\ Personality$$

Your slice is the set of traits He's gifted to you and asked you to steward on His behalf. It's critical that you are aware of your slice—your authentic personality—because if you aren't, you'll feel ill-equipped to do the job He's given you as a mom.

And trust me, He's got specific things in mind for you to do. As Ephesians 2:10 says, "For we are God's handiwork, created in Christ Jesus to do good works, which God prepared in advance for us to do."

The brilliant thing about your slice is that it allows you to do some things very well—in fact, better than most. You might have a keen eye for detail and a knack for analysis that the rest of us can't touch. Fantastic! Your family is blessed. But that God-given ability comes with an evil twin, a corresponding limitation, which explains why you're horrible at networking and speaking in front of groups.

That's the nature of a slice—it comes with signature strengths and annoying weaknesses, all known and understood by God when He chose it for you. Remember, He never created you to be everything to everyone. Instead, God designed you to be someone specific, a slice of His image, to the someones He placed in your life.

Identity Is Different Than Personality

Before we go any further, I need to stop for a moment and make an important distinction regarding identity and personality, because they are different things.

All humans on the planet bear God's image, whether they believe in Him or not, which means they have been wired with unique personalities that will endure over their lifetimes.

But for those of us who believe in Jesus as our Savior, we also have an identity in Christ. For example, as a believer:

You are a child of God.

You are the bride of Christ.

You are a friend of Jesus.

These identity statements (and twenty others like them found at the end of this chapter) are eternal truths about who you are as a believer in Christ. They will not change or ever be revoked. You belong to God and your identity found through Him secures your place in His family. It's your highest and most holy calling, a privilege that cannot be overstated, but one that doesn't describe all that you are and all that you can be.

At least it didn't for me.

I became a Christian when I was fifteen years old. I stumbled into a youth group meeting, planted myself on a worn-out couch (the kind you only find at youth group meetings and you're pretty sure harbors a communicable disease), and I've never been the same since. Not because I came down with the plague, but because I became a new creation.

Who was this brand spanking new creature? Someone who, according to my youth group leader, was *forgiven* for every rotten thing I'd ever done or would do. Someone who was *saved* from my sin and my shame. Someone who would one day go to heaven. Phew! He told me that the Holy Spirit had moved into my heart to heal me, guide me, and change me from the inside out. It was a lot to take in.

Throughout the years, I immersed myself in God to learn more and more about my spiritual identity. I studied my Bible, participated in small groups, and prayed routinely. And yet, something was always missing.

I never felt special among Christians. I didn't know if or how I was unique, because after all, everyone in the room had the same spiritual identity. I existed as a generic daughter of the King, lost in a crowd where every girl was the bride of Christ, and Jesus was everyone's best friend.

Until I understood my slice. Learning about my personality showed me how I fit and where I was needed in the family of God. My distinction highlighted that I was important to Him, gifted by Him, and chosen for particular work.

Scripture started to come alive. I'd insert my name and what I knew about myself into certain verses, and *voila!* the message became profoundly personal. It was as if God had written the words just for me. For example:

"Before I formed you in the womb, *Dale*, I knew you, before you were born I set you apart" (Jeremiah 1:5, my paraphrase). Or Psalm 139:13–16, also my paraphrase:

> *Dale*, your frame was not hidden from Me when I made you in the secret place, when I wove you together in the depths of the earth. I saw your unformed body before you were born. All the days of your life, *Dale*, were written in My book and ordained for you before one of them came to be.

Wow! The God of the universe was talking to *me*, with my driven nature and mom jeans. (I hear they are back.) He liked me. He loved me. He made me, just the way I am, for good reason. I was still in the process of discovering my purpose, but knowing my slice enabled me to move forward with more confidence.

It elevated my self-concept and allowed me to see myself as God saw me, that divine self-awareness.

And make no mistake: Because I'm made in God's image, I'm a little bit like Him.

I'm authoritative and productive because God is authoritative and productive. I act and move quickly because God acts and moves quickly. (You'll learn just how you are like God in Chapters 5, 7, 9, and 11).

I am my Father's daughter.

That's who I am. And so are you, in the way of your own slice.

But you need to be careful because beneath your strengths lurks a lie. It's a lie that can rob you of your identity, kill your confidence, destroy your true worth, and keep you from living up to your full potential before God. Your lie is specific to your Authentic Mom Type, so every mom of that type must face it at some point. Chapters 5, 7, 9, and 11 will make you aware of your lie, the truth that will set you free, and the spiritual discipline needed to get you there.

Your Potential Through Authenticity

Our goal as believers is to do life with Christ and become like Him. To act like Him, speak like Him, and love like Him. Identity in Christ allows that to happen. It gives us the opportunity to be like Him, more and more each day.

Certainly, we can grow to be like Jesus in many ways, but not in all ways. Jesus was born to a virgin (that's not our story), led a sinless life (that's definitely not our story), and "in Christ all the fullness of the Deity lives in bodily form" (Colossians 2:9) (that's not our story either). *What that means is that Jesus was the only human to get all the slices.* As the Son of God, He, too, is the whole pie.

As you grow into His likeness, strengthening your relationship with Him through Bible study, prayer, and time with His people, you'll grow more fully into your slice. "As we become more and more like Christ we become more uniquely our own true self."[4] Your strengths will get stronger and your weaknesses will get weaker when you are "on God."

But this doesn't happen by osmosis.

Richard Rohr reminds us, "We already have image (personality); we choose likeness."[5]

I hate to be a buzzkill, but it's true.

You're not going to just bump into the likeness of Christ or stumble upon your full personality potential by accident. You'll need to choose it, making the time to know and understand your design; the ways you uniquely reflect God. You'll need to decide whether or not to surrender your personality to Him, allowing His Holy Spirit to inhabit your gifts and transform your flaws.

It's up to you.

But I can tell you that it's a decision you'll never regret.

Once you make this decision, you'll learn to live at full strength. This is the "life to the full" (John 10:10) that Jesus offers us.

There is, however, a catch.

Abundant life, as it turns out, isn't for everyone.

It's not for your shiny self—the mother you've polished up to flawless perfection who never makes a mistake and always knows just what to do. It's not for your ideal self—that stronger, smarter, better version of you that you know you should be as a mom. And it's not for your false self—the pretend persona you put out there, in real life or on social media, to please your kids, your husband, or other moms.

No, the prettied-up versions of you are not invited.

But the real you is.

The authentic you.

It's important here that I define what I mean by authentic because I see it as two things. First, being authentic involves a *humble* posture, a vulnerable acknowledgment of what is real in your life right now. I call this your little "t" truth. Ninety-four percent of the moms I surveyed said they wanted to be more authentic. They long to be free to share what is true about themselves without pretense, performance, or perfection. They want to let their muffin tops fly free. Well, maybe not that much.

This is your stark-naked, raw self: *I'm stubborn. I'm critical. I don't follow through.* Often these admissions, if you're brave enough to go there, involve personality weaknesses. These are qualities you dislike about yourself and would prefer to hide because you're secretly afraid that something is wrong with you when, in fact, nothing could be further from the truth. Weaknesses are simply strengths taken to the extreme. (We will talk much more about this in the even chapters on your Authentic Mom Types.) They are to be expected for every mom who shares your type. When confessed openly, in humble authenticity, God will remove the shame from your weaknesses, forgive you, and then fill you. Peter speaks to all believers when he says, "Humble yourselves, therefore, under God's mighty hand, that he may lift you up in due time" (1 Peter 5:6). What looks and feels low (humble authenticity), God honors and lifts high.

The second aspect of authenticity is noble authenticity, because being authentic is also a *noble* stance. It's a proud recognition of what God promises is True (this is your big "T" truth) about you. It involves embracing all the potential God infused into your design and the greatness He imparted to you: His image, your slice, your strengths, His purpose. Not because of anything you've done, but because of what He's done for you. This noble stance grants you permission to mount your high horse (the one you've always been told to get off of), to sit up tall, and to ride. This is who God made you to be.

Fellow moms, you've waited long enough.

It's time to ride.

It's time to live your authentic personality, in all its beautiful humility and gorgeous nobility.

It's time to see yourself the way God sees you, in the way He made you to be.

It's time to reflect your slice of His image and use it for God's glory.

It's time to find out what type of mom you are.

Identity Statements[6]

Matthew 5:13	I am the salt of the earth.
Matthew 5:14	I am the light of the world.
John 1:12	I am a child of God.
John 15:1, 5	I am part of the true vine, a channel (branch of Christ's life).
John 15:15	I am Christ's friend.
John 15:16	I am chosen and appointed by Christ to bear His fruit.
Acts 1:8	I am a personal witness of Christ.
Romans 6:18	I am a slave of righteousness.
Romans 6:22	I am enslaved to God.
Romans 8:14–15	I am a child of God; God is my Abba Father.
Romans 8:17	I am a joint-heir with Christ and share His inheritance.
1 Corinthians 3:16	I am a temple (home) of God. His Spirit lives in me.
1 Corinthians 6:17	I am joined to the Lord and am one in spirit with Him.
1 Corinthians 12:27	I am part of Christ's body.

2 Corinthians 5:17	I am a new creation.
2 Corinthians 5:18–19	I am reconciled to God and am a minister of reconciliation.
Galatians 3:26, 28	I am a child of God and one in Christ.
Galatians 4:6–7	I am an heir of God because I am a child of God.
Ephesians 1:1	I am a saint; I am a part of God's holy people.
Ephesians 2:10	I am God's handiwork.
Ephesians 2:19	I am a fellow citizen with the rest of God's family.
Ephesians 3:1, 4:1	I am a prisoner of Christ.
Ephesians 4:24	I am righteous and holy.
Philippians 3:20	I am a citizen of heaven.
Colossians 3:3	I am hidden with Christ in God.
Colossians 3:4	I am an expression of the life of Christ; He is my life.
Colossians 3:12	I am chosen of God, holy and dearly loved.
1 Thessalonians 1:4	I am chosen and loved by God.
1 Thessalonians 5:5	I am a child of light and not of darkness.
Hebrews 3:1	I am a holy sister, and have a heavenly calling.
Hebrews 3:14	I am a partaker of Christ; I share in His life.
1 Peter 2:5	I am one of God's living stones.
1 Peter 2:9, 10	I am a chosen people, a royal priesthood, God's own Possession.
1 Peter 2:11	I am an alien and stranger in this world.
1 Peter 5:8	I am an enemy of the devil.
1 John 3:1–2	I am a child of God. I will resemble Christ when He returns.
1 John 5:18	I am born of God and the devil can't touch me.
Psalms 23, 100	I am a sheep of His pasture; He cares for me.

CHAPTER 3

Take the Mom Test

The moment your child was born, you became a member of the IMA, International Mom Association. (Actually the IMA isn't really a thing. I just made it up.) You survived nine months of indigestion, insomnia, and hormone-induced insanity for this great honor. If you became a mom through adoption, surrogacy, or fostering, you're also in the IMA after surviving your own set of challenges.

Welcome to the club.

Back in 1996 when my first daughter arrived, I thought I was walking into a maternal sisterhood, a community of like-minded mothers with similar thoughts, feelings, and ways of doing things. I thought we'd all sit around in a kumbaya kind of way and agree on what was most important for our kids.

Boy, was I wrong.

Everyone was different.

There were tiger mothers, attachment mamas, and moms who were a hot mess. (That might have been me.) I met zen moms, cool moms, granola moms, and competitive moms. There were as many different moms as cereals in the breakfast aisle at the grocery store. And I found myself scratching my head, like I often do in the cereal aisle, as I asked myself, *What kind of mom do I want to be?*

Great news! You don't have to wrestle with that question because God has already given you a distinct personality as a mom. He's assigned to you a special slice of His image, crafted specifically for your family, uniquely designed to meet their needs.

So what type of mom are you?

Your Mom Personality

I group moms in these four personality categories: Stabilizers, Improvers, Connecters, and Doers.

Where did the thought of personality come from?

I feel certain that the acknowledgment of different personality types began the moment Adam and Eve looked at their sons, Cain and Abel, and said, "Who are these people and why are they acting this way?"

But the first *written* explanation of personality goes back to 350 B.C. when the Greek physician Hippocrates identified four temperaments (sanguine, melancholic, choleric, and phlegmatic) based on different bodily fluids. (What mom wants to claim a personality type with the word "phlegm" in it? Haven't we seen enough mucus to last a lifetime?) Your predominant body fluid, he believed, produced specific behavioral characteristics.

Thankfully, over the last few centuries, psychologists[7] have refined Hippocrates' original work, further researching and validating the four basic types, to create the understanding we have today (and it's no longer based on internal secretions).

The Authentic Mom Types I describe in this book have their roots in scientific and psychological research, but I've created four new labels to be both useful and relevant to moms today.

While you have characteristics of all four types, you'll find that you have a dominant slice that God chose and wove into your very DNA. This type is true to your core—no matter what life brings, your most natural inclination will be to respond according to your personality type.

Many moms have a major type and a minor type. This is fairly common and further defines your uniqueness.

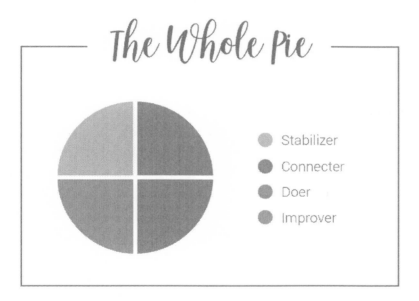

The Whole Pie

- Stabilizer
- Connecter
- Doer
- Improver

All four of these slices make up a whole image of God. If you're a Doer, you'll likely reflect God's action and His authority. If you're a Connecter, you'll reflect His communication and connection. If you're an Improver, you'll reflect His creative drive to make the world a better place. If you are a Stabilizer, you'll reflect His peace and faithfulness. Together "we, though many, form one body" (Romans 12:5), or pie, to display a full image of God.

Your children have a front-row seat to your slice. This is the portion of God's character that you'll demonstrate most fully for them, and the unique influence you'll have on their lives. Your mothering should be an expression of your slice. It's the best you have to bring them.

Let me provide a brief description of each type.

Stabilizer. The Stabilizer Mom is patient, pleasant, and people-focused. She's supportive, understanding, and always there to listen to her children. She likes routine and prefers to work behind the scenes. If she were a belly button, she'd be an innie due to her internal orientation. She keeps her thoughts and feelings to herself, and even internalizes the pain of others. She's soft-spoken and an amazing team player. Her family trusts her to be solid as a rock and counts on her to bring calm to the storms of their lives.

Connecter. The Connecter Mom is active, enthusiastic, and people-focused. She loves to talk, entertain, and make you laugh. She has a large social network because of her ability and desire to connect with others. She inspires her family with hope and optimism and has a knack for encouragement and persuasion. She's externally focused, an outie, wearing her emotions on her sleeve and sharing her thoughts (and I mean all of them) with those around her. She is creative, joyful, and super fun.

Improver. The Improver Mom is patient, precise, and task-focused. She values quality work and wants the very best for her family. She's got an eye for beauty that shows up in her artistic endeavors and organized plans. Like the Stabilizer, she's an innie—she thinks before she speaks and edits her ideas before she shares them. She's contemplative and cautious, and will analyze all options before moving ahead. She keeps her family out of trouble by keeping an eye on the details and instructing them to follow the rules.

Doer. The Doer Mom is active, energetic, and task-focused. She's a multi-tasking master who loves to get things done. She's independent, strong-willed, and leads her children with confidence. Her orientation is external like the Connecter, and she prefers her gifts and talents be used for public consumption. She has an amazing ability to make quick decisions, overcome obstacles, and take on responsibilities that other moms wouldn't attempt.

I can sum up these four types into four little phrases based on the way they do things:

Doers like things "my way."

Stabilizers like things "our way."

Connecters like things the "fun way."

Improvers like things the "right way."

You may recognize yourself immediately in these descriptions, or you may need a little more time. No problem. The remaining chapters will take you deeper into your type, and help you understand how to live in partnership with God so you can live in the fullness of who He created you to be.

It's time!

You can take the online test (five minutes, nine questions) at www. YourAuthenticPersonality.com/mom-test. After the test, you'll immediately know your type. Or you can take the written test on the next page. In that case, you'll put a check mark by each word that describes you, both strengths and weaknesses. And I'm not talking about what you *can* do. Most every mom I meet can *do* and *be* a lot of great things. For example, I can be patient when I'm well-rested and well-fed (and no one is having a meltdown in the produce aisle), but really, patience is not a great strength of mine. Nor is gentleness or peacefulness. I wish they were because they're beautiful qualities, but they're just not naturally me.

So be stark raving honest. Take this test like no one is looking. Only check the qualities that describe the truest essence of you when no one is watching.

Then tally up each column (strengths and weaknesses). Your highest number is your Authentic Mom Type.

What Type Are You?

Which type received your highest score?

Let's validate your score with a few clarifying questions that weren't on the test.

Q: Are you an asker or teller?
A: Askers are usually Stabilizers or Improvers. Tellers are Connecters or Doers.

Q: Do you prioritize tasks or people?
A: Doers and Improvers are task-oriented. Stabilizers and Connecters are people-oriented.

Q: Do you tend to be a public person or a private person?
A: Connecters and Doers are public in nature. Stabilizers and Improvers are private in nature.

Q: Do you lead with truth or grace?
A: Doers and Improvers lead with truth; they represent the firm side of God's love. Stabilizers and Connecters lean toward grace; they show us the soft side of God's love.

Q: Are you more comfortable with thoughts or feelings?
A: Stabilizers and Connecters tend to be "feelers." Doers and Improvers rely upon facts and data.

Your Authentic Personality Test

Put a check by the words that best describe you. They should NOT be words that explain what you **can** do, but what you most **naturally** do. I know, it's hard, but try to be honest. Tally each column including strengths and weaknesses in your total. The highest number is your major Authentic Personality type. The second highest number is your minor Authentic Personality type. Most of us have both a major and a minor. Watch out for major/minor blends that include Connecter with Improver or Doer with Stabilizer. These often indicate a personality mask. If all four of your totals are fairly even, you might be a Stabilizer. For more information, read *What's Your Mom Type: Discovering God's Design for You.*

Stabilizer

STRENGTHS	WEAKNESSES
__ diplomatic	__ easily overwhelmed
__ kind	__ conflict avoider
__ loyal	__ resists change
__ patient	__ enabling
__ peaceful	__ indecisive
__ flexible	__ indifferent
__ quiet	__ lazy
__ gentle	
__ comfortable	
__ friendly	
__ steady & stable	
__ supportive	
__ humble	___ total

Connecter

STRENGTHS	WEAKNESSES
__ optimistic	__ lacks follow-through
__ popular	__ fears rejection
__ outgoing	__ people pleaser
__ social	__ interrupter
__ adventurous	__ shallow
__ encouraging	__ forgetful
__ inspiring	__ late
__ fun	
__ funny	
__ talker	
__ lots of friends	
__ influential	
__ energetic	___ total

Improver

STRENGTHS	WEAKNESSES
__ accurate	__ fears making a mistake
__ creative	__ defensive to criticism
__ orderly	__ perfectionistic/critical
__ private	__ analysis paralysis
__ planner	__ negative
__ sensitive	__ unforgiving
__ precise	__ rigid
__ respected	
__ detailed	
__ knowledgeable	
__ values learning	
__ careful & cautious	
__ appreciates quality	___ total

Doer

STRENGTHS	WEAKNESSES
__ decisive	__ control freak
__ organized	__ impatient
__ multi-tasking	__ bossy
__ brave	__ rude
__ confident	__ self-sufficient
__ in charge	__ can't relax
__ direct	__ argumentative
__ responsible	
__ powerful	
__ mover & shaker	
__ action-oriented	
__ problem-solver	
__ goal driven	___ total

Your Authentic Personality™ www.YourAuthenticPersonality.com / YourAuthenticPersonality@gmail.com © 2018 Dale Wilsher. All Rights Reserved. Your Authentic Personality is a registered trademark of Dale Wilsher.

Q: Do you move fast or slow?

A: Stabilizers and Improvers move more slowly, both in the way they walk and in their reactions to circumstances. Connecters and Doers move quickly, in their actions and in their abilities to make decisions.

Each Authentic Mom Type chapter is written as if you were *only* that type, a pure version of one. In my experience, that rarely happens. As I mentioned before, most moms have a major and a minor type that create an authentic blend. That minor type can cover a multitude of sins. It can add a relational focus to a mom who's all about tasks. It can help balance her pace or her preferences for public or private life. It can smooth rough edges and add additional capabilities to her list of strengths. It's important, so please read through all the chapters to get to know *all* you have to offer. You may notice repetition in the descriptions. You might be tempted to skip through them, but please don't. Reminders are always good.

What do you think about your mom type? Do you like it?

As for me, I've never met an Authentic Mom Type that I didn't like.

But some moms love their type, and others don't. (Remember, it took me years to actually like my type.)

Maybe you've been a behind-the-scenes woman all your life (Stabilizer or Improver), but wish you were more lively and outgoing. Or maybe you feel like you're too talkative and silly (Connecter) or too honest and direct (Doer), and you wish you could be different. Perhaps you prefer solitude and silence, but then feel guilty because you're not more social. It seems that the grass is often greener on the other side of the personality fence. My hope is that every mom who reads this book will not only know but love her slice of God's image.

Slice Bias

I want to make sure you get to your true type, because there are obstacles in your path. Two roadblocks that could get in the way of an accurate result are slice bias and masking.

It is common to wish you were someone other than who you really are. As we discussed earlier, we're a culture that constantly compares ourselves to others, so we end up feeling "less than." When we become blinded by the brilliance of other types and lose sight of our own beauty, we develop what I call a slice bias.

What's a slice bias?

A slice bias is a tendency to prefer one slice of the pie over another slice.

I see it all the time in personality books. The very tool that you'd expect to be a sanctuary for all types is more often a pep talk for extroverts and a lecture for introverts. Authors applaud personalities that are large and loud and underestimate the value of the quieter types. Susan Cain, hailed for making introversion the "new black," says this in her book, *Quiet:*

> Introversion—along with its cousins sensitivity, seriousness, and shyness—is now a second-class personality trait, somewhere between a disappointment and a pathology. Introverts living in the Extrovert Ideal are like women in a man's world, discounted because of a trait that goes to the core of who they are.[8]

I also see a slice bias in the church, where women have historically been pressured to operate as grown-up versions of "sugar and spice and everything nice." It seems like our religious institutions prefer that we conform to a man-made image (theirs) rather than the one we were originally intended to have (God's).

Missie, a mom of two, says, "The message I hear at church is that Christian mothers should be pleasant, well-mannered, quiet, and obedient. That's our box and we should all fit in it. I've never been encouraged to live uniquely or be myself, if those qualities don't fit in the box."

Women at church are often socialized to display the feminine qualities of people-oriented types (Connecters and Stabilizers) such as softness, hospitality, and caregiving, while moms who are naturally direct, assertive, and task-oriented (Improvers and Doers) are encouraged to tone it down.

"I'm not talking about lighting my hair on fire and pounding shots of tequila," says Missie, "but I'd love to feel more freedom at church to express who I am."

Me too, Missie. Me, too.

Regardless of who squelches your inner you—your own inner critic, the culture you live in, or the people in your church—remember that God has already spoken in the way He designed your slice.

He created your inmost being.

He knit you together in your mother's womb.

Your slice has been fearfully and wonderfully made.

Please don't minimize your design. Can you imagine how much that would grieve the heart of God? Your slice matters. Your slice is needed in the whole pie.

Masks Are Not Just for Halloween

Most moms see their test results, turn to the chapter that describes their type, and say, "This describes me to a T." Some, however, say, "This score, this mom type, doesn't describe me at all." Still others aren't aware that their results are artificial rather than accurate.

I've worked with many women whose personality scores did not accurately reflect their authentic design. For a variety of reasons, they scored themselves as they believed they *should* be or *could* be, rather than who they are.

This is called masking.

Masking is the process of displaying a false or man-made image by covering your true identity. Like the actors in ancient times, you wear a mask to become someone else. And you may not even know you're doing it. Masking isn't always conscious. But it does happen every day, especially for women.

We mask in our relationships.

We mask to conform to social pressures and unrealistic expectations, like when other moms expect us to entertain the masses when we'd rather just read books. We can mask when our job requires us to develop skills that are way out of our wheelhouses. We can mask when we find ourselves in hard marriages, doing anything and everything to improve the relationships. These adaptations become masks when we accept them as who we are.

We mask in our formative years.

During this stage of development, life-changing factors cause us to hide our true selves. Parental slice bias causes problems when your sibling's qualities are favored over your own. Or when your mom or dad think they're supposed to make you into *their* image, instead of God's image. (Watch out for this in the way you parent. It's easy to do.) Criticism, neglect, and any type of emotional, physical, or sexual abuse cause us to mask.[9] These experiences force our true selves into hiding as we cover up who we are so that we can cope or survive the events of childhood.

Laura, a client and mom of two, didn't believe she was a Connecter because she had always maintained a perfectly ordered home with everything in its place (classic Improver tendencies). Laura cleaned obsessively, not because she *delighted* in cleanliness and order (the sign of a true Improver), but because she desperately wanted to please her Improver mother. Laura cleaned well not because it was a natural inner motivation, but because she just wanted her mother's approval. People-pleasing starts as parent-pleasing, and can cause confusion as to our authentic selves.

If you think you might be masking, read through *all* of the chapters to see which one best describes the true you. Look back at your early years and evaluate what you were like before you began to cover up your true self. Ask your spouse or a good friend, who knows you well and likes you lots, to share the qualities they see in you. And, of course, pray. God has designed you with a singular type or a particular blend. That truth cannot be shaken. Let Him lead you to the authentic version of you that He made in the beginning and will delight in at the end.

As you can see, several factors affect the reliability of test results. They are self-administered, after all.

I wish I could have a one-on-one coaching session with you, look over your test score, and spend a bit of time getting to know you to make sure your test results are accurate. But because that's not likely to happen, at least not today, I'd like you to answer two questions before you turn to the chapter that describes your type.

- Do you have a slice bias? Do you secretly value other personality types over your own? If so, be aware that your results may be skewed. Slice bias is based on elevating one set of traits over another, acknowledging the benefits of some characteristics, but not others. If you've ever wished you were different than who you actually are, please read through all of the chapters to understand the advantages of each type. Pray and ask God to help you see yourself the way He does, embracing the value of your personality type and the reflection of His image that only your slice brings to the pie.

- Were you "gut-level" honest in your answers to the test questions? Or is it possible that you "masked" your answers by responding with what you can do or should do (on a good day)? Sometimes we are more authentic on the bad days. If it's possible that you masked your real responses with "good" responses, ask God to reveal your true self as you prayerfully read through the book.

It's time to dive deeper into your slice! As you go forward, I pray that the Holy Spirit guides you into all truth about your slice. May He teach you things you don't yet know as a mom and remind you of things about your authentic self that you might have forgotten. I hope each chapter feels personal and meaningful and blesses you and the generations to come.

I close with this prayer for you.

May today there be peace within.
May you trust that you are exactly where you are meant to be.
May you not forget the infinite possibilities that are born of faith in yourself and others.
May you use the gifts that you have received, and pass on the love that has been given to you.
May you be content with yourself just the way you are.
Let this knowledge settle into your bones, and allow your soul the freedom to sing, dance, praise and love.
It is there for each and every one of us.
Saint Teresa of Avila[10]

CHAPTER 4

Stabilizer: The "Steady-As-She-Goes" Mom

A soft-spoken mom who holds her family steady, promotes peace and harmony, prevents breakdowns and unwanted changes.

I've got three little words for you.

I. See. You.

I see your stability, your faithfulness, and your caring heart. I see your gifts of observation and your ability to listen well. I see your thoughtfulness, your tender mercy, and your helpful attitude. I see the way you accept others and put up with all manner of things. I see the balance and steady rhythm of your life.

Because you aren't demanding, others sometimes miss seeing you. They take you for granted, like the air they breathe or water they drink, because you are ever-present but never any trouble. People who are insecure and thrive on being seen tend to dismiss your strengths as average and ordinary when, in truth, they are nothing short of significant and exceptional.

The truth is this: We desperately need you.

Without you, we'd all go our own way.

Without you, we'd be contentious, rude, and grumpy.

Without you, we'd all feel rushed and exhausted.

Without you, we'd be restless, jittery, and full of angst.

Without you, the world would be cold and harsh.

Without you, we'd be left alone in our pain and misery.

Without you, we wouldn't feel seen or heard.

Your Top Five Superpowers

While you may not be faster than a speeding bullet or more powerful than a locomotive, the kindness with which you patch up a boo-boo and the sacrificial care you offer to meet all of your family's needs inspire admiration in the eyes of other moms.

As you read through your strengths, please take your time. As I already mentioned, others sometimes take you for granted—and you know this is true—but you often take *yourself* for granted. Most Stabilizer clients I work with miss the magnificence of who they are and what they bring to their families. I ask that today, just today, you see *yourself*.

Let this list affirm you. Let it declare the beauty of your design.

But let this list also stir you. Use the questions at the end of each description to help you consider the ways you might use each superpower for even greater good in the lives of your children.

1. You're a diplomatic mom. If you were a country, you'd be Switzerland. Nonpartisan and neutral. When your kids come to you yelling, "Trevor just hit me!" or "Caroline's hogging the bathroom!" your impartial stance allows you to act as an effective go-between in the heat of the moment. When your neighbors send a nasty text complaining that your bushes are growing through their fence and your radon vent is blowing their way, you don't get defensive. You mediate. You compromise. You reconcile. You have a knack for finding the middle ground that puts an end to bickering, complaining, and hostile disputes.

In what ways has your diplomacy blessed your family?

2. You're a nurturing mom. All moms care for their kids, but your instinct for nurturing goes above and beyond the rest of us. You naturally respond to your child's needs with warmth and kindness. Hungry belly? You're happy to cook. Skinned knee? You've got a Band-Aid. Scary nightmare? You're willing to lie down with your child. Anything to help. You reassure them, soothe them, and console them. There's almost nothing you won't do for your children—picking them up when they cry, taking lunches when they forget, making beds when they're late. You'll sacrifice money, sleep and, if necessary, the shirt off your back, to provide your family with a loving and caring home.

How has your ability to nurture your kids enhanced their lives?

3. You're a loyal mom. You stand by your family, for better, for worse, for richer, for poorer, in sickness and in health, until death do you part. You do. Your kids come before everyone else. "Family first"—that's your motto. You keep your promises. If you tell your kids they can live in your basement until they are forty-five, you'll honor your word (uhmm . . . might want to be careful there!). You're also faithful to the traditions passed down from previous generations. If Grandpa George believed in evening walks and homemade ice cream, you'll do your best to keep those customs alive. Your kids can rest in the security that you'll always be there for them, faithful and true.

How have your children benefitted by your loyalty to them?

4. You're a patient mom. You may not think that you are patient, but compared to every other type, believe me, it's true. You take time for your children, more than most. You'll spend the entire morning doing crafts or the whole afternoon at the playground because you've been gifted with a pace that allows you to accept delays and distractions, and simply hang out. You value companionship and the enjoyment of spending time with others, so you're able to be present and available to your children. While the rest of us rush our kids to bed at night (because we just can't take it anymore), you read one more book, give them one last kiss, and deliver one last cup of water. You are slow to anger, slow to speak, but quick to listen. You rock.

How does your patience make your kids feel loved?

5. You're a peaceful mom. You're a natural tranquilizer and an antidote to anxiety in your family. The atmosphere of your home is quiet and serene. My shoulders relax just thinking of you. When your sons shove each other in the produce aisle, you peacefully defuse the tension. When your husband brings home a surprise dinner guest, you take it in stride. When your favorite eyeliner breaks in the middle of getting ready, when your kids draw all over the new couch, and when your boss invites you to his office for your performance review, you take the good with the bad without getting your feathers ruffled. You keep calm and carry on.

In what ways have you created peace in your home?

As a mom, you have opportunities every day to lead and influence your family using your five superpowers.

These superpowers greatly influence your leadership style. Did you know that you have a distinctive leadership style? You do. Let's look at that now.

Servant Leader

"I'm just not a leader," said Sara, mother of two boys ages eight and ten. "That's why I struggle so much now that my husband isn't here and I have to make all the decisions." Sara's husband, an officer in the military, had just left for a year-long deployment to points unknown (at least unknown to me or she'd have to kill me).

"Why don't you think of yourself as a leader?" I asked.

"My husband's the real leader. He gets stuff done. He's structured. He's good with tasks. He handles the discipline because the boys respect his authority. I feel inept trying to lead. I just want someone to tell me what to do."

"Sara, how would you describe the leadership style of Jesus?"

"He was a servant leader."

"And that's a good thing?" I prompted.

"Oh yes, of course."

"How would you define a servant leader?"

"Well, a leader who serves others. He doesn't need recognition. He's sacrificial. He gives up his rights. He's willing to do the hard work for the good of us all."

"That sounds an awful lot like you."

"I guess you're right. I do like to serve. I've sacrificed a lot of sleep, what's left of my career, and basically all of my personal time to take care of my kids. I've never thought that my service qualified me as a leader, but maybe it does."

It took Sara a few more sessions to fully understand her unique leadership style, but once she did, she became more confident and intentional in leading her two children according to her special slice.

As a Stabilizer Mom, you have a different way of leading than your husband, and anyone else who isn't your type. Let's look at the type of leader you are.

You're an approachable leader. Your children follow you because you are pleasant and friendly. Your warm smile and heartfelt attention put them at ease and make them feel comfortable. They share their ideas, their opinions, and their feelings with you because you're easy to talk to and your door is always open. When you ask them about their day, you listen, *really* listen. When they talk about the fight they had with their best friends, you don't jump in to solve their problem for them. Instead, you gently encourage them to work it out. When they share their opinions about their favorite band, baseball team, or fashion trend, you're curious, choosing acceptance over judgment. And when they don't want to talk, you give them space and grace, because you understand.

You're a balanced leader, providing the stability your family needs. Just like a big toe (the one they cut off ancient kings when they lost in battle. Gross, I know, but I am not making this stuff up. Check out Judges 1:7), you serve as a solid foundation to keep your family upright and even. You buffer the fluctuations of your children's blood sugar. You moderate their mood swings and calm them down. And when it comes to whose turn it is to play on the Xbox, you're the great equalizer, making sure things are fair and equitable.

You're a dependable leader, establishing regular routines for different times of the day: morning routine, bedtime routine, carpool routine. Everyone knows what to expect and that you'll be there. When you coach the swim team, you show up on time, every time. When it's your turn to bring snacks for homeroom, the teacher knows you'll be there. When others bail on a project, you hang in. You're trustworthy. Everyone can count on you. In a world filled with empty promises, that's a pretty astounding trait.

You're a team leader. This is one of your greatest leadership qualities. You believe that everyone matters. Everyone has a part to play, especially the underdog that others ignore. "We're all in this together," you like to say. You encourage shared goals. You clean the garage together. You get everyone to help with dinner and eat together. You take family vacations and play family games that work for all ages and stages. You consider the needs of each child but act in the best interest of the family unit. You celebrate individual victories but also see it as a win for the entire family. You want a group consensus before making a decision. You are community-minded rather than individually motivated.

You're a humble leader. You put the needs of others above yourself. You value each member of your family and honor them with dignity, respect, and kindness. No job is too small or insignificant. You grab a sponge and show your son how to clean a toilet so he learns a new skill. You roll up your sleeves and help your daughter with number theory, algebra, and geometry, hoping it all comes back to you. You readily admit your own mistakes and expect that your kids will make plenty, too.

Be encouraged, dear Stabilizer. Your five superpowers and leadership skills are desperately needed in a world filled with frantic panic. But just because you make life better for all of us doesn't mean that bullets will bounce off your chest. Yes, you are a supermom, but like the rest of us, you have your weaknesses. Let's look at those now.

Stabilizer Mom Kryptonite

Superpowers come with inherent weaknesses. Sad but true. (Unless, of course, you are Wonder Woman, who is an anomaly even in the superhero world.) Take the Black Panther, for example. While strong and mighty in his suit, out of it he's open to injury and even death. Then there's his loyalty to his home country, a preference that blinds him to the needs of the world at large. And, of course, he's susceptible to electrocution. Poor guy. And you, Super Stabilizer Mom, have your own vulnerabilities, too.

Your weaknesses are actually your strengths gone wild. What started as a good thing can become a bad thing when it's taken too far. Read on to see what I mean.

But please remember that your weaknesses are necessary because they bring you to your knees and remind you of your brokenness (that's a good thing). Your weaknesses force you to run to God and seek forgiveness (that's a *very* good thing). Your weaknesses keep you humble, which is the recipe for an authentic self, calling for you to admit what is true about you right now (that's a *very, very* good thing).

I've put these weaknesses in the form of questions because, more than likely, these are the things you ask yourself when you're ensnared in a weakness. See if you can relate to these questions.

Why do I feel so responsible for others? You just want to help, to make things easier for those who you love. But often your supportive nature crosses the line into enabling behavior. Enabling is doing for others what they can and need to do for themselves. Admittedly, this is tricky. As a mom, you must constantly assess and reassess if brushing teeth, making lunches, or waking your children up in the morning are things that you should do, or they should do. If you don't reassess, you send a message to them that they aren't capable of handling responsibility, becoming independent, or doing hard things.

Galatians 6:2 tells us that we should, "Carry each other's burdens." The word "burden" is better translated as "boulder" to define the size we are talking about here. As a mom, you're called to carry the burden when it's too big for one child to bear. But in Galatians 6:5, we read this: "for each one should carry their own load." At some point, your child can carry that burden, and you need to let him. Be careful about getting in the way of your child's development by keeping him or her from the consequences of behavior. Let them figure stuff out; it will teach them to problem-solve. Let them be late; it will teach them to set an alarm, so down the road they won't get fired from a job for tardiness. Let them do without the Legos they won't pick up. You're not being mean. You're building competence, strength, and autonomy.

Why can't I make a decision? You don't like making decisions, big or small. Why? Sometimes it's because you lack self-confidence. Other times it's because you simply don't like change—change creates stress, and you hate stress. Sometimes the potential outcome of making a decision is so bad that you procrastinate or shut down. Truth be told, you'd rather take orders than make them. You want others to be happy, so you go along with their decisions. But, sometimes, this is not wise.

One of the greatest gifts and responsibilities that God has given us is free will, the ability to choose. Joshua 24:15 says, "Choose for yourselves this day whom you will serve."

The best thing you can do is to ask God to help you with every decision you make. God eagerly desires to help you make choices. John 16:24 says, "Until now you have not asked for anything in my name. Ask and you will receive, and your joy will be complete."

Why don't I stand up for myself? You're a lover, not a fighter. To a fault. Others tell you, "You're being taken advantage of," but you don't see it that way. You tell yourself that you're easygoing, tolerant, and lenient. You'd rather not make waves or hurt someone's feelings, so you shrug off conflict and keep your mouth shut. But as we've heard many times, "The only thing necessary for the triumph of evil is that good men (and women) should do nothing."[11]

Let me just tell you plainly. There is a time to take a stand. Ephesians 6:13 says, "Therefore put on the full armor of God, so that when the day of evil comes, you may be able to *stand* your ground, and after you have done everything, to *stand*" (italics mine).

As one of my Stabilizer clients used to say, "There comes a time when I need to put on my big girl pants."

She's so right.

Let your voice be heard, even if it might ruffle a few feathers. I'll tell you a secret. Because of your gentle nature, no matter what you say, it's unlikely that anyone will feel ruffled by you. So take the risk and stand up for yourself.

Why am I so overwhelmed? As a mom, you're hit by a million things every day, and the sheer volume of it all leaves you dazed. Email notifications. Kiddo questions. Household errands. Family issues. Endless appointments. And then there's the stuff. You know the stuff. The sports gear. The arts and crafts. The plastic games (did you ever think your home would be filled with this much plastic?). Because you do best when you have a single focus, excess stuff stresses you out. You want to clear it out, but the potpourri in the corner came from Nana Glenna, sweet Nana Glenna. The gift subscription for the fifty *Cooking Light* magazines came from your mom. And the six tubs of baby clothes. Are you kidding? Your firstborn grew up in those. Your stuff is all tied to meaning and memory. How can you throw away Nana Glenna, your mom, or your firstborn?

"And so, crestfallen, he walked away. He was holding on tight to a lot of things, and he couldn't bear to let go" (Matthew 19:22 MSG).

It may be time to purge. Let your kids pick their top five stuffed animals and give the rest away. Box up "outgrown" or "unused" items, put them in your car, and drop them off at the thrift store. Take photos of your child's art projects, with them in the pictures, then throw the art away. Ask your mom to stop sending toys or *Cooking Light*. Hold on to the memories that you have of Nana Glenna, but let the potpourri go.

Why do I sometimes feel indifferent? Yes, you're relaxed and laid back (love that!) but you can cross the line into laziness and lethargy. Yes, you're a keen observer (bravo!) but you are susceptible to living life as a passive bystander rather than as an active participant. Of the four personality types, you are most susceptible to indulging in "nothing time" such as binge-watching your favorite Hulu show or scrolling through Instagram for hours on end. While you may believe that you are conserving your energy, research has shown that, after thirty minutes of nothing time, it is no longer producing a restful effect. And the greater danger is this: When you get sucked into nothing time, you disengage from family activities, relational challenges, and even parental discipline. When this happens, your kids can feel neglected and unworthy of your time and effort.

"If anyone, then, knows the good they ought to do and doesn't do it, it is sin for them" (James 4:17).

I know you desperately love your family, so muster up your energy and be intentional about connecting with them. Ask them questions. Don't just watch the games they play; participate with them. Change your title from "observer" to "active participant" when it comes to your kids. Remember, they need you. We all do.

I want to switch gears for a moment and talk about another important issue that you must face if you are going to live life authentically before your family.

What's My Trigger?

Every mom has a trigger, a switch that, when flipped, can morph her into "scary mommy." What does "scary mommy" look like for you as a Stabilizer?

It's not pretty.

Like a smoldering volcano that simply must erupt because of the churning tension within, you suddenly blow. You mutter hateful words (so unlike you). You explode with volatile irritation (your kids look at you like they don't know you). Then you withdraw, feeling embarrassed and helpless against the force of your emotions.

What is it that triggers your mommy meltdown?

Let me tell you straight up.

Your main trigger is **conflict**.

When your kids have a screaming match, you get triggered. When your daughter refuses to take her medicine. When your husband complains about the mess in the house. When a mom from school falsely accuses your son of hurting her son. When your mother-in-law calls, wondering why you haven't called her. When someone, anyone, has a temper tantrum.

You hate it. No, you loathe it.

Conflict, the loss of harmony, stings you more than it stings other moms because of your design as a Stabilizer. It makes sense. Your abilities to hold things steady, keep people together, and promote a peaceful environment (your greatest strengths) are threatened by any form of conflict.

So how do you stop your trigger from changing you into scary mommy?

It's easier than you think. And it's as simple as this: Be aware.

When there's tension in a relationship—hostility such as arguments, differences, or disagreements—pay attention to the emotion rising in you.

At this point, you might be tempted to dodge the conflict. To go along to get along. To act nice, play nice, and be nice. But, before you do, think about this:

Did you know that the word "nice" is never mentioned in the Bible? In their book *No More Christian Nice Girl*, authors Paul Coughlin and Jennifer Degler say,

> A lot of what people call nice behavior is really fear, cowardice, and even sin in disguise. Many women are nice not because they truly care about other people, but because they fear conflict and rejection. That's not peacemaking. That's peace-faking.[12]

Please. Don't be a peace-faker. It's simply not true to who you are. In the moment of tension, stop.

Say to yourself: *I sense conflict.*

Admit*: It scares me.*

God does His best work when we name a problem and bring it out into the light.

Congratulate yourself for being real. Accept your humble and authentic state. Tell God that you need Him.

You can rise above your knee-jerk reaction, and instead, offer a divine response.

Ask God, *How do You want me to handle this?*

He might remind you that the person you're experiencing conflict with is a different personality type than you, with different needs and different priorities. Others see the world differently than you do, so they're not likely to agree with you. Seek to understand them and what they need in the situation. If possible, help them to meet their needs.

He might remind you that your child is hungry or needs a nap. With a little food and sleep, this too shall pass. He might encourage you to use your gift of diplomacy to bring about a peaceful solution. He might tell you that you need to set limits on bad behavior. You might need to speak up or stand firm.

He will most likely tell you to be a peacemaker, and that He will show you what to do and say.

Peacemakers aren't always nice, but they are kind. When peacemakers experience a problem, they go to work to correct, reconcile, and restore true peace in relationships. A peacemaker is courageous enough to voice her feelings in love and respect and to invite the other party to do the same.

You need to be brave enough to risk speaking the truth in love so that you can bring the peace of God into your relationships and our world. Jesus, the ultimate peacemaker between God and man, was killed for not playing nice. Don't ever settle for nice, when you can make peace.

A Cup of Self-Kindness

Recently, while waiting for a flight to take off, I was pleasantly surprised and genuinely entertained by a flight attendant who was fed up with the canned safety instruction speech.

> In the event of a sudden loss of cabin pressure, oxygen masks will drop down in front of you. Stop screaming, grab the mask, and place it over your face. If you are traveling with small children, we are sorry. Secure your mask before assisting with theirs. If you're traveling with more than one child, pick out the one that you think has the most earning potential and place the mask on that one.

Don't you just love airline personnel with a sense of humor?

As a Stabilizer with a natural bent toward caring for the needs of others, your instinct will always be to place the oxygen mask on someone else first, regardless of earning potential. *But if you don't take care of yourself first, you could end up passed out in the aisle, and unable to help.* How can you take care of the world if you don't take care of yourself?

I ask that you see the following self-care practices—like your oxygen mask at 60,000 feet—as necessary to your life. Please understand that these are the acts that will help you survive.

Smoke a peace pipe. Before you start wondering if I'm a little more "out there" than you thought, no, I'm not suggesting that you buy a pipe and smoke it, or anything else. I am suggesting that you try mimicking a few of the calming actions associated with smoking the peace pipe. First, sit quietly. Now close your eyes. Then inhale deeply into the core of your being—you're not inhaling smoke, but the peace of Christ.

Peace is like air for you. You must have it.

Jesus is the Prince of Peace. He alone can give you the kind of peace you need, not the shallow, temporary peace the world gives, but a much greater, unshakable peace (John 14:27). Colossians 3:15 says, "Let the peace of Christ rule in your hearts, since as members of one body you were called to peace." Turn this verse into a daily, *personal* prayer. Before you even get out of bed, ask God to fill you with His peace. Ask Him to help you constantly surrender your heart and mind throughout your busy day so that His peace, the kind that passes understanding, may rule.

Peace is one side of a coin; silence is the other. Silence may be golden for others, but it's platinum for you. Mute your phone. Take the batteries out of your kids' musical toys. Turn off the TV. You need quiet spaces and quiet places to bring your body, soul, mind, and spirit back into harmony. You need a quietness of spirit and inner tranquility that transcends financial worries, marital struggles, and children who won't brush their teeth or comb their hair.

Curl up on the couch. Nothing fills your cup like comfort. Give yourself permission to snuggle up with cushy pillows. Slip into 1,200-thread-count sheets. Pull on a comfy sweater, fleece-lined vest, or warm jammies. If your shirt is itchy, send it to Goodwill—it's not worth the irritation it causes you.

Fill your tummy with comfort. Mac and cheese. Homemade chicken soup. Anything with frosting. If you like chocolate, buy the good stuff.

Comfort your body. Take a bubble bath. Ask one of your kids to give you a back rub. Give yourself a foot massage. Let yourself be comforted so that you will be able to comfort others.

Take a nap. With a more subdued energy than the other types, it's imperative that you get the rest you need. I napped almost every day until my youngest went to school. I didn't get much done and had hardly anything to add to my section in the Christmas letter, but I was in a much better place to love my kids for the rest of the day. If you work outside the home, make time to nap on the weekends. It doesn't have to be long; just fifteen minutes of quiet shut-eye can refresh you. Power naps are the way to go. The important thing is to give yourself quiet space for a few moments in the middle of the day. Don't apologize for needing this. Instead, spend the quiet moments thanking God that, as you are quiet, He can fill you up with the energy you need for the rest of your day.

Speak affirmations to yourself. It might seem obvious, but whatever you feed, grows. This isn't just a physical truth; it's a spiritual one, too. If you'd like to see yourself the way that God sees you (and I sure hope that you will), then you must feed yourself with His thoughts and His words.

During a season in my life when I became aware of how negatively I spoke to myself, I begged God to take my thoughts captive and replace them with His truth. Here are some things He said to me: "Nothing is wrong with you. You are just right for me. You are beautiful. You are brilliant. You are mine." I wrote these affirmations on my bathroom mirror so I could feed myself with them every day. I spoke them out loud while I washed my face. I spoke them silently while I brushed my teeth. I starved my inner critic and made it obedient to Christ.

Choose your favorite affirmations. Maybe you like something from the list above. Maybe it's your list of superpowers or leadership skills. Whatever is true, noble, pure, and lovely—"think about such things. Whatever you have learned or received or heard from me, or seen in me—put it into practice. And the God of peace will be with you" (Philippians 4:8–9).

Have a family movie night. Gather everyone around the TV and watch your favorite flick. When you are with the fam, it pushes the needle of your happy meter to high, especially if hot, buttered popcorn and Milk Duds (my personal favorites) are added to the mix.

If the family is dispersed, invite a close friend over for a cup of tea or a game of cards. Enjoy the companionship of those you love. You don't need quantity when it comes to people, just a few long-standing friendships with others who know you, value you, and have your back.

Remember, not everyone is like you. If your best friend and husband are different personality types, they may not have your intense need for peace, comfort, or rest. But don't neglect these needs for yourself. Take care of yourself, and we will be blessed because you will be at your best to do what you do so well.

The next chapter will take this a step further. You'll learn how your design as a Stabilizer Mom mirrors God and what you have been gifted to reflect. You'll also learn how to overcome the lie that you're most likely to believe about yourself and how God wants to inhabit your slice and infuse it with His divinity.

CHAPTER 5

Discover God's Design for Stabilizers

Who are your people?

That is the question that every guest who attended our Southern family brunch had to answer.

I noticed that some guests (mostly those from the area) didn't miss a beat and quickly responded with answers like "the Spauldings from Brookhaven Drive" or "the Connors from Valdosta." They knew their replies would provide a type of ancestral GPS, telling us who and where they came from.

The day I brought a guest from my Midwestern hometown, I froze, right there over the congealed salad, because I realized that I had not prepped him for the question, and he was hoping to make a good impression. My eyes grew wide as Aunt Vivian leaned his way. *Here it comes*, I worried.

"Darling, who are your people?" she asked.

He tilted his head, thought for a second then smiled as he replied, "the Norwegians?" Everyone at the table giggled. That's a lot of people.

How would you answer the question: *Who are your people?* With your street name, hometown, or family tree? Concerned that it doesn't say much about you? Not to worry.

There is something much more original to you than your last name or your childhood home—it's your dignity as an image-bearer of God. You may not have been given a big name or an impressive heritage, but you have been given an inheritance, an irrevocable gift, that is part of your Father's blessing over you.

It's your slice, your portion of God's riches, bequeathed to you so you can carry on His legacy and reflect His nature to the world.

Your slice is His stamp of approval imprinted on who you are and who He made you to be. It's a visible declaration of His favor toward you. He likes who you are. He made you this way.

When God looks at you, He smiles because you remind Him of Himself. Let me tell you how.

Your Inheritance

Like you, God is the glue holding it all together. God is the mysterious force that sustains every element in the universe. "When the earth and all its people quake, it is I who hold its pillars firm" (Psalm 75:3). Like the forces He created—gravity, electricity, and nuclear forces—God holds both the natural and the spiritual worlds together.

He also sticks with us. "I am with you always," says Jesus, "to the very end of the age" (Matthew 28:20). He is "a friend who sticks closer than a brother" (Proverbs 18:24) and a God who will never "leave you nor forsake you" (Deuteronomy 31:8).

Like you, God is a helper. This is no throwaway gift. "God is our refuge and strength, an ever-present help in trouble" (Psalm 46:1).

He makes it easier for us to do what He has called us to do because He offers us His omnipotent, omniscient, and omnipresent aid. He brought His great power to bear against the enemies of Israel to help his people overcome in battle. He used His divine wisdom and knowledge to help Joseph and Daniel interpret the dreams of kings and rise to positions of influence. He continues to provide help to His people around the globe at all times and in all ways to carry out His divine plans and purposes.

Like you, God loves comfort. In Psalm 23, God comforts David with His rod and His staff. In Isaiah, He comforts His people with His words. Known as the God of all comfort, the source from which all relief and encouragement flow, God "comforts us in all our troubles, so that we can comfort those in any trouble with the comfort we ourselves have received from God" (2 Corinthians 1:4). At the end of time, Jesus will comfort us all as He wipes away every tear from our eyes and destroys death, mourning, crying, and pain. I can't wait.

Like you, God is steady. Jesus Christ is the same yesterday, and today, and forever. God doesn't change His mind (Numbers 23:19) or anything about Himself (James 1:17). His word "is eternal; it stands firm in the heavens" (Psalm 119:89). God is immovable, unshakeable, and completely dependable.

Like you, God sees. My favorite name of God, given to Him by Hagar, an Egyptian slave girl (non-Christian from out of town), is El Roi. It means "The God Who Sees." As a Stabilizer Mom, you know what it means to feel invisible—unappreciated, undervalued, and sometimes unworthy—because much of what you do goes unseen. But God sees you. He sees you doing dishes, folding laundry, or staying up all night with a sick child. He sees your hurts, your heart, and your love for your family, even when no one else does. He sees it all. His loving eyes are always upon you.

Like you, God is a team player. He's not just one person. He's three-in-one—Father, Son, and Holy Spirit—the heavenly team. He's got angels on His team, too, a heavenly host. And He surrounds us with a great cloud of witnesses (Hebrews 12:1), believers who have died and now cheer on the team. He created His people to be the "body of Christ," a team of many members working together for God's purposes.

Doesn't it make you feel good to read about the many ways that you are like God? Doesn't it make you stand a little taller? Feel a bit more confident? I sure hope it does.

God wants you to know of His loving intention behind your design, but He also needs you to be aware that your slice has an Achilles' heel, an area of weakness, that is vulnerable to a lie. This lie can remain dormant for years, rendering you clueless to its existence. But make no mistake. It is extremely dangerous. So dangerous that, if it's not weeded out, it can lead you astray and away from the One you reflect.

The Lie

Karin is my real-life best friend. She's a labor and delivery nurse and Stabilizer Mom of her three children. She's always been patient and deeply caring. Once a foster mom to seven different children, she now fosters newborn kittens, usually several at a time, and boy are they cute. Karin is calm and calming. She's talked me down from the "I'm-having-one-of-those days-and-I-can't-do-it-anymore" moments on more than one occasion. She's pleasant and friendly; she can get along with anyone.

Ten years ago, her husband, Terry, was given a terrifying diagnosis: early onset Alzheimer's. He was fifty-four. At the time, their children ranged in age from seven to seventeen. It was the most difficult thing I've ever seen another mother endure, especially a Stabilizer whose home had always been a sanctuary for peace and harmony.

At that time, Karin and I ran together in the wee hours of the morning before our families woke up, because we were desperate for exercise and it was the only time available. Most of the time it was dark, making it easy to talk freely, so Karin would share from the heart.

"Terry's always been so friendly and laid-back. I've always loved that about him. But he's becoming more and more agitated every day. He's argumentative and angry, not just at me, but at the kids, too. I'm trying to protect them from seeing this side of their dad. I'm trying to protect Terry from knowing what is happening to him. I'm trying to keep the conflicts to a minimum, but I just can't seem to stop them. Nothing is easy. Everyone's hurting. My home is pure chaos."

Her words reminded me of Naomi, a Stabilizer client, whose son had just been diagnosed with Asperger's syndrome. She, too, wanted to protect her son from the difficulties of his disease, which is why she agonized over whether she should even tell him about it.

"I don't know if he can handle it," she admitted. "I don't want him to be labeled. I want him to be comfortable in his own skin. I want his social interactions to be easy, and they aren't. One day I will have to send him out in a world that does not understand him. I just feel so guilty that I can't make this better."

Although different situations, Karin and Naomi share the same doubts about who they are because they just don't feel like themselves. In their own minds, they wonder,

Who am I if I can't provide a safe and peaceful environment at home?
Who am I if I can't alleviate the pain of those I love most?
Who am I if I can't be patient and caring?

Do you see what has happened to these moms? Somewhere along the way, they believed a lie, one that every Stabilizer must address at some point. The lie they believed is this: ***I am more valuable when I am helping others.***

The problem is that their *identities* had become tangled with their *personalities*. They've confused their values with their gifting. Their worth became attached to the strengths of their slice rather than their places in the family of God.

Have you ever believed the lie?

On some level, haven't you felt that you are more acceptable and lovable when you are supporting, caring, and keeping the peace? Do you ever feel that your value comes from accommodating others and making sure everyone gets along? Do you assume that when people are comfortable and at ease, God is more pleased with you? Do you wonder if God is disappointed in you when you're not able to help everyone in your life?

Enough is enough. It's time to pull this lie out from the shadows, wrestle it to the ground, and send it to the pit of hell where it belongs. You are too precious to God to continue living this lie.

No matter what anyone says or how they respond to you, your value and your acceptability before God are not based on your ability to alleviate suffering. Your value and acceptability before God are based on who you are—His daughter—*not* on what you do.

Yes, God gave you the strengths of the Stabilizer slice—your empathy, calm, and your servant's heart—but He wants to inhabit those qualities and infuse them with His divine power. He wants to make them better, greater, and even more fruitful.

How does He do this?

God prunes (John 15:2). He cuts away the greatest assets in your life and renders them ineffective and seemingly useless, as He did in Karin and Naomi's lives, but during these times, I believe He's doing some of the most significant work He'll ever do in your heart. You see, God must remove anything in which you've placed your confidence that is false or flimsy, even if that means rescinding the strengths of your slice. Anything that you love more than God, things that make you feel more acceptable, more presentable, more likable, or more loveable—must be dethroned. It's only when you are completely naked, stripped down to your most authentic self, and fully accepted in that state, that you will know your value rests in His love and not in your strengths.

It hurts, this cutting away. And yet it is so necessary. He goes deep to lay a new foundation. He removes the old structures upon which you've instinctively built your worth and value (whether you knew you were doing that or not), and replaces the lie with an important truth. The truth is this: **Jesus delights in you *not* because you are helpful, but because you are *His*.**

The Journey to Truth

One morning, Karin met me at the end of the block for our morning run, with a smile on her face. "Can I borrow your vacuum cleaner today?" she asked.

"Sure. What happened to yours?"

"We got into a fight and I won," she giggled.

Karin didn't have a reputation for taking down household appliances, so I asked her what prompted the skirmish. As we began to run, she shared.

"I've been trying to hold it all together for so long, to keep things normal for my kids, to protect their innocence, to keep them from all the ugliness in the world, but it's not working. And then I read my *Streams in the Desert* devotional this morning."

She pulled out a little piece of paper from her pocket and, under the light of the street lamp, read what it said.

"Those who suffer most are capable of yielding most; and it is through pain that God is getting the most out of us, for His glory and the blessing of others."[13] She put the paper back in her pocket and turned toward me with tears in her eyes.

"Dale, God is telling me that I have to surrender my pain and the pain of my children to Him. This is not going away, and I can't buffer any of us from it. God doesn't need me to keep us from suffering. He's not punishing me or them." She continued, "God doesn't always keep us from trouble," her voice now shaking but resolute. "He is *with* us in trouble. This morning, in the wake of my vacuum cleaner meltdown, I finally realized that God isn't mad at me for not bringing peace, He just wants to *be* our peace. And He's going to use all of this, as difficult as it is, for our good and His glory."

Karin's focus as a mom had been to provide her kids with an idyllic childhood—a loving family, great friends, and a safe neighborhood. She had wanted to love them, comfort them, and shield them from the harsh realities of life. But God wanted more for them than that.

Romans 5:3–4 tells us that we can "Glory in our sufferings, because we know that suffering produces perseverance; perseverance, character; and character, hope."

As a result of the deep suffering they were experiencing, Karin was seeing perseverance and character in her kids. They weren't superficial, as often happens in suburban bubbles where life is easy and pain is fleeting. Brody, her oldest son, became one of the youngest sergeants in the army. Her youngest son, Ben, normally the quiet and shy type, stepped up to protect a mentally disabled classmate from the aggression of a bully. Bergen, her daughter, became an "old soul" offering the type of compassion and understanding normally found in mature adults.

And they are seeing hope. Not all at once, because their story is far from over, but they get glimpses. Not all of our stories are wrapped up nicely with a bow. Some are messy. Some are still in process. Some are deeply sad and hard. But God is still good. And He is definitely at work.

Your Slice "on God"

If you would like to see what the Lord can do with your strengths, what your slice looks like "on God," you'll want to embrace the same spiritual practice that made such a difference in Karin's life.

Surrender.

Interestingly enough, *surrender* isn't a word you'll find easily in the Bible. It's only used one time in the New Testament, in reference to the people handing Jesus over to Pontius Pilate to be crucified (Luke 23:25), and infrequently in the Old Testament. Surrender is mainly a military term, so it's used to describe the relinquishment of armies or territory to an enemy force.

The concept of surrender, however, is woven throughout scripture, as the true way to follow God.

Surrender is laying down your own agenda. Surrender is relinquishing what you consider your own. Surrender allows God to be the authority, not only in your life, but in the lives of your children.

While surrender may feel helpless and even hopeless, neither of those is true. Surrender is the means to true victory, because the moment you surrender your desires, your concerns, and even your children to God, He is in control. They are now in His hands and He will be victorious.

If you're new to surrender, let me suggest three practical tips that may help you establish this daily practice:

1. Trust fall into God's arms. I'm sure you've seen the exercise. An individual turns her back on a crowd. The crowd moves in close. The woman crosses her arms over her chest, closes her eyes, and falls backward, unsure of what will happen, but trusting they will catch her. It's called a trust fall. It's what it looks and feels like to surrender yourself to God.

When you make the decision to trust in Christ for your personal salvation, you close your eyes (usually but not necessary) and pray, trusting that He hears you. Which he does. You trust that what you've read in the Bible or heard from others is true. Yes, He is the way, the truth, and the life. Yes, He is crazy in love with you. Yes, He accepts you, forgives you, and saves you the moment you ask Him to. Then you fall backward into His strong, loving arms because He is there to catch you.

Trust falling into God is both a momentary experience (like the one above) as well as an ongoing process. Each and every day you will need to surrender to His priorities, His direction, and His will for your life.

2. Trust in God's heart for your kids. While peace and ease may seem best for your children, if God allows hardship and difficulty, you can know that He is on it. His ways are not your ways, but He is always on their side (Psalm 118:6).

Before they were your children, they were God's. Before He formed them in the womb, He knew them. Before they were born, He set them apart (Jeremiah 1:5). God is your child's heavenly parent, who, believe it or not, loves them more than you ever will.

This is so important because, if you don't release your children to God, it will affect your own relationship with Christ.

> Anyone who loves their father or mother more than me is not worthy of me; anyone who loves their *son or daughter* more than me is not worthy of me. . . . Whoever does not take up their cross and follow me is not worthy of me. Whoever finds their life will lose it, and whoever loses their life for my sake will find it (Matthew 10:37–39, italics mine).

But if you do surrender your children to God, you will receive great blessing.

> And everyone who has left houses or brothers or sisters or father or mother or wife or *children* or fields for my sake will receive a hundred times as much and will inherit eternal life (Matthew 19:29, italics mine).

3. *Embrace the purpose in pain.* Hebrews 12:11 tells us, "No discipline seems pleasant at the time, but painful. Later on, however, it produces a harvest of righteousness and peace for those who have been trained by it."

There is purpose in pain. God uses it to grow us and our children up.

When a butterfly begins to emerge from its chrysalis, it must wiggle and struggle for hours to release itself from the cocoon. It jerks, it gyrates, it seems to writhe in pain. If you've ever watched this happen, it's difficult to sit there and do nothing. But if you try to help, you will hurt the butterfly (and the officials at the butterfly museum will take you into custody). In order for the butterfly to move fluid from its bloated body into its weak and delicate wings—to enliven them and make them capable of flight—the insect must struggle.

Through the journeys of our lives, I've had to watch my daughters struggle a great deal. It's been excruciating at times, knowing that I could not make it all go away. But there were things that I could do. And you can do, too.

Be fully present with your children, but don't be overly protective (i.e., a helicopter parent).

Be concerned for your children, but don't treat them with kid gloves all the time. They can handle hard stuff if you let them.

Be attuned to your children, but don't take their problems on as your own. Listen to them. Empathize with them. Support them. And trust that God is allowing this struggle for their good and His glory.

And if you do these things, our all-loving, ever-present God will renew their strength and cause them to soar.

Now, let your Father tell you how He feels about you and the beauty of your slice.

My Stabilizer Daughter,

You are loyal to the core, steady, trustworthy, faithful, and tender hearted. I wove these qualities into you from birth so that you might reflect My character to those who desperately need to see evidence of these traits in a world that is often faithless and unstable, a world where hate and violence quickly erupt.

Others love you because, in you, they find someone who offers comfort, care, and dependability. You bring peace and calm in moments of chaos. You are loving and quick to serve—it is second nature to you because I created you this way. These are the same qualities that my Son, Jesus, demonstrated to the world.

My people desperately need the qualities I have placed in you. But sometimes you hide because you aren't comfortable being the center of attention. I understand this because I created this humble quality in you. But that does not mean I want you to be invisible. You are a vital part of what I am doing in this world. At times, I will ask you to be vocal, to boldly declare a message I will give you. You will need to speak and serve in a way that may require you to be in the spotlight. But do not be afraid. I will give you the words to speak. I will inspire you with the right actions and responses. It will be the power of My Holy Spirit doing these things through you. This is an area of growth for you. Will you trust Me?

Will you ready your heart and mind for those moments when I ask you to stand and speak up? Daughter, open wide your mouth and I will fill it. Look to me as your constant Helper, your constant partner. Allow Me to help you keep peace, and to make peace through you. Spend time with Me each day. Listen as I speak to your heart. Read and study My Word. That is another way in which I will speak to you.

At times, I will call you to bring peace in the midst of chaos. But remember, you do not need to be peace for anyone. I am Peace. I will ask you to bring comfort in the midst of grief. But you are not their comfort. I am the Comforter. Don't confuse what I ask you to do with who you are. Your identity is secure because you are My daughter. Follow My lead. Sometimes I will withhold peace and comfort in a situation because I have a higher purpose in mind. Other times, peace is what is required. There is a time for peace, and a time for war. Walk alongside Me and I will speak to you in these different times. Leave the responsibility of all things squarely on My shoulders as you grow into the fullness of who I have created you to be.

With All My Love,
Your Father

CHAPTER 6

Connecter: The "Social Butterfly" Mom

A fun mom who attracts others, establishes communication, creates relationships, and builds community.

I'm captivated by you Connecters.

As I Doer, I simply don't have many of the strengths that come naturally to your type.

Let me tell you what I love about you.

I'm crazy about your insane love for people. You've never met a stranger because everyone is your friend. And no wonder.

You influence and inspire us with your creativity. You're bursting with ideas you can't wait to share, and your unbounded energy and contagious enthusiasm infuse us with excitement for new possibilities.

You're chatty in a happy sort of way. Yes, you sometimes talk before you think—you fail to filter—but your honesty is refreshing. Your candor blows us away.

You crack us up, like no one else, with your hilarious stories and outbursts of humor.

I love your heart for fun and the way you celebrate life's little moments by making every day a party. YOU LIVE YOUR LIFE IN CAPS LOCK! And you LOVE exclamation marks!!! You've been given a gift in the way you so generously express your emotions and your feelings, making us all feel loved and cherished.

You remind me of a sunflower with its happy, yellow petals and smiling face tilted up to the sun, thriving with light and brightness. Who would tell a sunflower to get serious or stop looking so cheerful? No one! Because sunflowers make us smile simply by being what God created them to be.

I'm so grateful that God made this slice of His image that is you.

You may not think that what you bring to the table is so special. You may think that other moms are just like you.

No, they're not.

The Institute for Motivational Living reports that only about eleven to twenty percent of people are what I label as Connecters. You have many gifts that are desperately needed in your community and in the body of Christ. Join me as we look more closely at the top five superpowers God has woven into you as a Connecter Mom.

Your Top Five Superpowers

While you may not be faster than a speeding bullet or more powerful than a locomotive, the enthusiasm with which you flip pancakes and the charisma that draws everyone to you inspires admiration in the eyes of other moms.

As you read through your strengths, please take your time.

Let this list affirm you. Let it declare the beauty of your design.

But let this information also stir you. Use the questions at the end of each description to help you consider the ways you might use each superpower for even greater good in the lives of your children.

1. You're an OPTIMISTIC mom. For you, every day has the potential to be the Best! Day! Ever! You live on the sunny side of the street where good things happen and every cloud has a silver lining. When your kids start to sink, you buoy them right back up by reminding them of the hope ahead. When they start to complain about people or problems, you reframe their negativity with positive affirmations. You help them see the opportunity in every difficulty. At your house, the future is bright.

How does your optimistic mindset influence your children?

2. You're an EXPRESSIVE/COMMUNICATIVE mom. Your kids know your voice, your ideas, and your feelings on most any subject because you tell them. You instinctively know how to use language to share your emotions and opinions, but you also take into account what others think and feel. Because of you, your family is informed. Connected. Engaged. Your natural charm and entertaining stories capture your children's attention, which provides you with a wonderful platform to teach and train them in the way they should go.

How does your ability to communicate help your family?

3. You're a SOCIAL mom. Relationship is king for you. Community is key. The ability and desire to do life with others is part of your genius. You host parties, plan festive celebrations, and accept every invitation that comes your way. You encourage play dates and clubs, activities and teams. You want your kids to mix with and get to know all kinds of people. Using your gift of hospitality—and your Costco-sized stockpile of plates, decorations, and delicacies—you welcome your kids' friends, their parents, and guests of all kinds into your heart and into your home.

How do your social connections bless your family?

4. You're an ADVENTUROUS mom. You have a sense of play that makes life fun! You fly by the seat of your pants, transforming dull and mundane trips to the grocery store into mini-adventures. You entertain. You amuse. You bring joy. Who wouldn't want to sit shotgun in your minivan? Your daring and delightful nature paves the way for new experiences, groundbreaking highs, and a fresh sense of wonder for the whole family.

How is fun a blessing to your family?

5. You're an ENCOURAGING mom. You are the official family cheerleader, root-root-rooting for your home team. You chant and clap from the sidelines because you are their biggest fan. You're the spirit leader, invigorating your daughter's mood, and infusing pep into your son's steps. You applaud every success and boo each setback, inspiring them to do their best. Your pompoms are always ready to provide support, energy, and enthusiasm.

What does your family do differently because you encourage them?

As a mom, you have opportunities every day to lead and influence your family using your five superpowers. These superpowers greatly influence your leadership style.

Did you know that you have a distinctive leadership style? You do. Let's look at that now.

Follow the Leader

"I don't think of myself as a leader, at least not when it comes to my kids," admitted Chelsea, a client who is a Connecter and a mom with three young kids. "You should meet Ashley, my sister-in-law. She homeschools her children and they start every day with a ten-minute Bible lesson that focuses on how to build integrity in their lives."

"And you think that's what makes Ashley a good leader?" I asked. "To provide structured learning for her kids?"

"Yeah, I'm just not that organized. It may sound lame in comparison, but I think it's really important to play with my kids. Just this morning, we played I-spy games and Candy Land. My kids love 'the mommy game' where they tuck me into bed and make my lunch. That is hilarious. We play soccer and hide-and-seek outside."

"Chelsea," I said, "you just described several ways that you *lead* your children through play. You help them problem-solve with board games. You develop their motor skills through physical activity. You help them build their language skills, social skills, and imagination through make-believe. You are doing the work of a leader, just in your own way."

"Hmmm. I never thought of it that way, but when you say it like that, I do sound like a leader."

It took Chelsea a while to fully understand her unique leadership style, but once she did, she became more confident and intentional in leading her family according to her special slice.

As a Connecter Mom, you have a different way of leading than other moms. Let's look at the type of leader you are.

You're the FUN leader, the kind we love to follow. Whether you're nurturing, teaching, or disciplining your kids, you keep things light and friendly. Spontaneous and lively. Casual and informal. You serve all activities with a wink and a smile.

You're an ENERGIZING leader, caffeine for the whole family. You're always on the go, constantly tossing around new ideas, and changing course at a moment's notice. Your contagious excitement for life infuses energy into each one of your children. You rev their engines in the morning. Refuel them in the afternoon. And generate enthusiasm all the way up to bedtime. Fanfare, parades, and emotions of any kind are all part of the process. Your tribe responds because they believe what you've told them: "We can do this!"

*You're a **PERSONAL** leader,* showing interest in all aspects of your children's lives. You ask questions and meet their friends because you want to know them better. You build strong relationships with each child through open and honest communication, frequent hugs, and their favorite snacks. (You're smart. You know that kids are suckers for tasty snacks.) You're approachable, so your children talk to you. They confess their failures knowing you'll go easy on them. They bring you their problems because they know you care.

*You're a **POSITIVE** leader,* building morale with your upbeat attitude and smiley-faced emojis. You expect good things to happen and they usually do. You're the queen of PMA, positive mental attitude, counting your blessings and believing in miracles. You show your children how to see the good in every situation and how to turn a frown upside down.

*You're an **INFLUENTIAL** leader.* Your web of connections benefits your children. You always know someone (or someone who knows someone) to help your kids grow forward. Got a daughter failing math? No worries. Your friend Tina has a sister who has a niece who is a genius with equations. Is your son's soccer game suffering? Your hairdresser has a client who was a former soccer coach at the local college. You have thousands of Facebook friends and phone contacts at your fingertips. You're forever connecting someone in need with someone who can answer that need because of your influential network of contacts.

It's true! You are amazing with your five distinctive superpowers and your unique style of leadership. But that doesn't ensure that bullets will bounce off your chest! Yes, you *are* a super mom, but like all of us, you have your vulnerabilities. Let's consider these now.

Connecter Mom Kryptonite

Superpowers come with inherent weaknesses. Sad but true. (Unless, of course, you are Wonder Woman, who is an anomaly even in the superhero world.) Just look at Deadpool. He drives everyone crazy with his incessant talking. And even though he's funny, he's mentally unstable. He's also a bit of a glutton, especially for Mexican food. And you, Super Connecter Mom, have your own vulnerabilities, too.

Your weaknesses are actually your strengths gone wild. What started as a good thing can become a bad thing when it's taken too far.

But wait, there's good news. Every weakness you have is actually a divine opportunity to learn dependence upon God.

Your weaknesses bring you to your knees and remind you of your brokenness (that's a good thing). Your weaknesses force you to run to God and seek forgiveness (that's a *very* good thing). Your weaknesses keep you humble, which is the recipe for an authentic self, calling you to admit what is true about you right now (that's a *very, very* good thing).

I've put these weaknesses in the form of questions because, more than likely, these are the things you tend to ask yourself when you are ensnared in a weakness. See if you can relate to these questions.

Why am I so concerned about what other people think? Making people happy is your strength, but it can also be your downfall. For example, you say yes when you mean no. You overpromise and over-commit. You just want others to like you. When they do, you get to connect, enthuse, and inspire (all your greatest hits). But when people reject you, you try your best to become whatever it takes to live up to their expectations, even if that means abandoning the authentic you. Luke 6:26 warns against this. "There's trouble ahead when you live only for the approval of others, saying what flatters them, doing what indulges them" (MSG).

Instead of people-pleasing, I encourage you to make God-pleasing your goal. Seek the applause of One—God—rather than the praise of the crowd. He's the one who made you a Connecter and He knows that this is hard for you. Seek to follow His voice instead of the human voices of pressure and expectation. Continue being considerate of others but don't lose the courage to be your authentic self.

Why can't I just keep my mouth shut? Your expressive nature and desire to communicate can get you into trouble. You go to lunch with a friend and you're so excited to catch up that your mouth starts running a mile a minute. By the time the meal is over, you've done most of the talking. Sound familiar? As a woman with Connecter as my minor type, I do this all the time. It's embarrassing. But worse yet, in my desire to verbally process everything that's ever happened to me, I hurt my relationships.

"The more talk, the less truth; the wise measure their words" (Proverbs 10:19 MSG).

Ask God to get your attention when you interrupt others. When you notice it, admit it and apologize. Take a deep breath and simply listen. Ask more questions. Let others enjoy the blessing of being heard. Connection is a two-way street. Whether your conversation is on the phone or in person, make sure that others get as much "air time" as you.

Why is it so hard for me to finish what I started? You rock the start of a project, but follow-through is not your strong suit. You get jazzed to redo the dining room. You buy the paint and cover one wall, but before the project is done, you lose your steam because the last steps feel tedious and wearisome. You find a great diet, stock your frig with kale and riced cauliflower, but fall off the wagon three days later because you're too busy to give it your full attention. You've said it a million times: "If you don't pick up your backpack, it's going in the garbage." But do you ever do it? No.

"The end of a matter is better than its beginning" (Ecclesiastes 7:8).

Don't bite off more than you can chew. Commit to activities that you can reasonably complete. Tell others about your goal, whatever it is. Put it on social media. Get a sponsor, a friend who you will call when you fall off the task wagon or who will join you in your objective. Ask your kids to hold you accountable. Find ways to make the project fun 'til the bitter end. Picture how happy everyone will be when you've finished strong.

Why do people think I'm shallow? When your best friend has been attacked by a shark or buried alive in a box and all you can think to say is, "It's all good," we've got a problem. Believe it or not, a positive mental attitude can go too far. Too much optimism can sugarcoat reality, minimize pain, and overlook heartache. It can seem fake and phony and detached from real life. Sometimes your children need you to dive into the deep end of their feelings instead of splashing around on the surface. At times, they need you to sit with them in their struggles instead of immediately cheering them up.

"Laugh with your happy friends when they're happy; share tears when they're down" (Romans 12:15 MSG).

Before you rush your son or daughter to happy, pause and share their suffering. Walk with them through the ugly emotions of fear, anger, and sadness. In the animated Disney movie *Inside Out*, we see the damage that can be done when joy runs the show and keeps sadness at bay. Only when the main character, Riley, experiences a full range of emotions is she able to connect to herself and her family in an honest and healthy way.

Why am I so scatterbrained? Because both your mind and your physical world are in constant motion, you sometimes fail to stop and remember where you put important items. Your phone. Your car keys. Even your child (most Connecters have forgotten their child at least once). There's just not enough brain space to always remember everything—people's names, that extra task you promised to do at church, or the meeting with the accountant that, while it was important, lacked the fun-factor to stay in your brain.

Your crowded mind also forgets the time, causing you to constantly run fifteen minutes late. Well, sometimes it's more like an hour late.

But who's counting?

Actually, everybody else.

Remember, "Love is not rude" (1 Corinthians 13:5 NCV).

You see being late as a forgivable and understandable offense, but others see you as not valuing them or their time, which can create tension in your relationships. Try to understand how your actions impact those who wait for you rather than squeezing in one more phone call or noble action.

What can help you be more focused? Take full advantage of the phone that you carry with you everywhere. Use the reminders feature to create lists of all kinds: grocery lists, to-do lists, Christmas-buying lists. Use your calendar feature to input birthdays or special events. Set the alarm feature to remind you one day or one hour before events. Also, try to take advantage of the handy-dandy timer feature to limit the amount of time you spend on social media, or to signal you to stop any activity that tends to be a time-sucker.

So those are your top five weaknesses. Could you relate to the questions? Maybe you thought, *Oh, this is so true, and I hate this about me.*

No! Please don't feel that way.

If you were perfect, no one would be able to connect to you. When you are slick and shiny, without any imperfections, people tend to slide right off.

Connection requires grit.

We need a surface to hold onto that acknowledges human failings and weaknesses. We need to know we are not alone. We need a safe place to be our humble, authentic selves as we grow into our noble, authentic selves.

Your weaknesses will also provide the traction needed to connect more fully to God.

They will draw you to Him as you seek His grace and mercy and teach you to rely upon Him for His strength. These weaknesses present wonderful opportunities for you to grow, to change, and to give glory to God as He refines you.

Beware of Scary Mommy

Every mom has a trigger, a button that, when pushed, can morph her into "scary mommy." The trigger for each personality type is different, but some of the emotions that emerge are similar.

You feel it welling up. Jealousy. Insecurity. Anxiety.

You're worried that you could blow. You don't want it to happen, but sometimes it does. You scream. You swear. (I admit, when triggered, I've heard some choice vocabulary coming out of my mouth that I didn't know I had in me. Please don't tell my mother.)

You wonder if there's something wrong with you. Right?

First, let me tell you that you are normal. Yes, you get triggered—but no, nothing is wrong with you.

Then what? What's the cause of this mommy meltdown?

Let me tell you straight up.

Your main trigger is **rejection.**

When your kids ignore you, tune you out, or say mean things to you, they trigger you. When your husband refuses to listen to your ideas, he pushes your button. When your mom withholds her praise and disapproves of the way you do—well, everything—you are triggered. Connection has been destroyed, and you feel that disconnect deeply. You hate it. No, you despise it.

Rejection, the loss of relationship, stings you more than other mom types because of your design as a Connecter. It makes sense.

Your abilities to attract others, establish communication, and build community (your greatest strengths) are threatened by any form of rejection.

So how do you stop your trigger from escalating into a mommy meltdown?

It's easier than you think. And it's as simple as this: Be aware.

When your son doesn't like you because you won't let him play in traffic, recognize the fear of rejection that surfaces. When your mother-in-law disapproves of your vegan lifestyle, or your best friend doesn't have time to get together with you, or your daughter closes her door and shuts you out, pay attention to the emotion rising in you.

Stop where you are.

Say to yourself, *I'm feeling rejected.*

Accept it.

Then ask God: *How do You want to meet this need for me?*

God might bring to mind a friend who you could call. He might give you an idea for how to meet new people. He might just want to sit down and connect with you Himself. One of the sweetest encounters I've ever had in prayer was when Jesus gave me a visual image of sitting down together on a lawn chair in the backyard of my parents' house, Him grabbing my hands and looking deep into my eyes, and saying, "Tell me how you're doing." That connection still brings tears to my eyes.

If you've experienced deep rejection in your past, those wounds need attention. If you feel unlovable or undesirable, chronically disconnected, hopeless, or even depressed, these are signs that you need to delve deeper into past events and understand how they may trigger you today.

The rejection of your past doesn't have to cripple you in the present. You can take a long, hard look at those painful moments for the purpose of bringing healing to the wound. First and foremost, look to God to heal you. Psalm 147:3 says, "He heals the brokenhearted and binds up their wounds." Ask Him to speak to your heart. He may want you to consider a life coach or a professional counselor who can help you deal with the rejection in a way that is healthy. By whatever means necessary, please pursue this. Your children will thank you. Scary mommy isn't their favorite mommy.

Treat Yo' Self

Self-care gets a bad rap because, too often, it's synonymous with self-centered and self-indulgent activities. Or it conjures up images of people lying around all day, doing nothing.

But you're a mom.

You never get to lie around.

You barely get to sit down!

So let me be perfectly clear about what I mean when I use the phrase *self-care*. Real self-care isn't selfishness; it's stewardship. It's taking care of what you've been given. Empty, exhausted, and in need of repair is not a good platform for effective parenting. That's why it's essential that we steward our bodies and minds, so we can take better care of our families.

Here are the most important things that you, as a Connecter Mom, can do to take care of yourself.

Give God a call! Your most important connection will always be to God, so talk to Him all day long. You naturally relate to God as a friend, so talk to Him like one. When you're driving to work, chat with Him about your upcoming day. I do this out loud so I look a little crazy, but *hey!* I'll probably never see those other drivers again. When you're vacuuming the stairs, tell Him what's bothering you. When you're confused about His will, ask Him. When you read your Bible, ask Him to make the words come alive on the page, as if they were written just for you. Before you call a friend, share your good news with Him, and offer Him thanks. Enjoy His companionship wherever you are. You don't need to sit down to pray. Just talk. This is your style of prayer—an ongoing conversation with God—so never stop praying (1 Thessalonians 5:17 NLT). Remember, with God there's no pretense, no need to impress. Just be your authentic self (ahhh, doesn't that feel grrrrreat?).

Girls Night Out! As a Connecter, you have a built-in need to be with others. This cannot be overstated. You need relationships. It's how you were made. If you're going to share your gifts of optimism, encouragement, and influence, you can't do that by yourself.

The truth is this: You. Need. People.

And not just your kids.

True, moms with older children (middle school or older) say that as much as fifty percent of their need to connect is met by their children.

But if you've got preschoolers, you need adults.

Failure to cultivate friendships of your own is dangerous because you will be tempted to treat your children as friends rather than be their parent, and you'll lose your ability to lead them well.

When you find yourself running low, phone a friend. When you've been holed up with sick children for days, get a babysitter and meet your peeps for coffee. If you're feeling unmotivated, get a buddy. Go to MOPS, say yes to invitations, and initiate play dates of your own.

And don't forget, church is a great place to be with others. Get involved in small groups. Join a Bible study, and you are twice blessed—blessed by connecting in new ways with God and with His people.

Try out that Pinterest recipe! Motherhood is often like the movie *Groundhog Day*, in which you live the same day over and over. This type of routine sucks the life out of you because, for you, variety is the spice of life.

As an extrovert, you have more receptors in your brain for dopamine, one of the happiness hormones. This means that to be happy, you need more dopamine than other moms do. Every time you *do* something or *see* something new, dopamine floods your brain, providing the necessary high to keep you feeling good and engaged.

Keep the happy hormones flowing by embracing your creativity.

Go to new places (a never-before-explored park, children's museum, or vacation spot). Meet new people at church, at the gym, or in your neighborhood. Bake a new dish. Plant a new flower. Pull out your hot glue gun, find something ordinary, and bedazzle it. One of my favorite ways to bring novelty is to rearrange the furniture. I just did it yesterday. My office feels like new and I didn't spend a dime.

Allow something new to spring up in you and you will be refreshed.

Laugh Out Loud! Some girls just want to have fun, but you, dear Connecter, *need* to have fun. A childlike spirit is crucial to your well-being. You need to enjoy what you are doing, to laugh, and to live in gladness of heart. Fun makes you more productive. It improves your relationships. It even increases your capacity for learning.

So when you do the dishes or fold laundry, queue up your favorite Spotify playlist. Tell jokes while you make dinner (even to yourself, if no one else is around). Play dress-up with your kids. Eat dessert. Have a tickle party. Go shopping (if your budget is tight, the Dollar Store is your friend).

Zumba! You have a crazy amount of energy coursing through your veins. If you don't burn it off, you'll be anxious, jittery, and (I'm sorry to have to tell you this) annoying to be around.

So move your body through exercise.

Go for a run or take a brisk walk *with a friend.* Take a spin class at a gym that offers childcare. When the weather's ugly, have a dance party in the family room. Run up and down the stairs, do some push-ups (we're all supposed to be able to perform as many as our age, and I admit I'm not quite there yet). Lunge around the kitchen.

Remember, not everyone is like you. If your best friend and husband are different personality types, they may not have your same needs for conversation, people, or fun. Don't let that deter you. Acknowledge your needs and take care of them. Steward yourself and the superpowers you have to share. Your family will thank you for it.

The next chapter will take this a step further. You'll learn how your design as a Connecter Mom mirrors God and what you have been gifted to reflect. You'll also learn how to overcome the lie that you're most likely to believe about yourself and how God wants to inhabit your slice and infuse it with His divinity.

CHAPTER 7

Discover God's Design for Connecters

I've always wanted to win the Powerball jackpot, a Mega Millions prize, or even some juicy scratch-off game. Haven't you? Even when I didn't want to admit I was falling for the official-looking, gimmicky Publisher's Clearinghouse mailings, I often imagined my look of surprise when the company representative rang my doorbell and presented me with a balloon bouquet and a six-foot check made out to me for a million smackers. I'm not picky. I'd even settle for a fat inheritance from a reclusive uncle I've never known but who considers me worthy of his riches.

As much as I love the idea of instant riches, there's not much chance it will ever happen because I never buy lottery tickets and I don't have any unaccounted-for relatives.

But there is an inheritance I've received—an irrevocable gift—that is part of my Father's blessing over me. It's your inheritance as well.

It's your slice, your portion of God's riches, bequeathed to you so you can carry on His legacy and reflect His nature to the world.

Your slice is His stamp of approval imprinted on who you are and who He made you to be. It's a visible declaration of His favor toward you. He likes who you are. He made you this way.

When God looks at you, He smiles because you remind Him of Himself. Let me tell you how.

Your Inheritance

Like God, you're a talker. You inherited your communication skills from Him. How do you think the sun, moon, and stars came into existence? By His spoken word. And He didn't stop there. He talked to Adam, Eve, Noah, Abraham, Isaac, Jacob, and Joseph. In fact, God spoke to our ancestors and through the prophets "at many times and in various ways" (Hebrews 1:1). He speaks to us today most commonly through His Word and through the indwelling presence of His Holy Spirit, but also through dreams, visions, nature, and impressions in our spirit.[14] According to John 16:12, God has much to say, just like you.

Like you, God is hilarious. Think about it. Do you think it's possible for God to create a platypus, a penguin, or a baby armadillo if He didn't have a sense of humor? Who would think to save His own prophet from drowning by "providing a huge fish to swallow Jonah" and then leaving him in there for "three days and three nights" (Jonah 1:17)? And who, but a joker, would think to call out a sorcerer named Balaam by speaking to him through his own donkey? That's right, the first and last comic standing is God.

God, like you, loves a good party. In the Old Testament, He proclaimed seven different festivals (old-school parties) that the Jewish people were to celebrate each year. In the New Testament, Jesus celebrated at weddings, banquets, and Jewish feasts. He urged His followers, "Let's have a feast and celebrate" (Luke 15:23), which might be why His first public miracle was turning water into wine. The final scene in the Bible points to a future celebration that all believers will enjoy—the wedding feast of the Lamb. God loves to host extravagant events for His family and friends, something that is second nature to you as a Connecter.

Another way that you are like God is that you love people. Not just Christians or folks who go to church, but people of every nationality, shape, color, and language. Loving people is as easy for you as breathing (other personality types—not so much). That's because, as a Connecter, relationship is what you are all about. Do you realize what an amazing God-quality this is? God exists in relationship. He is a trinity of three persons as one God (always a stumper if you think on that too long). God loves to be with His people, which is why Jesus is called Emmanuel, God with us. God loves being with you and He would do anything for you. In fact, He loves all people so much that He gave us the life of His Son, so we wouldn't perish, but have everlasting life (John 3:16).

Like God, you are also generous. You give, give, give, and you are happy to do so. You give your time to be with others. You give your money to those in need. You buy gifts and give them to your hairdresser, the cute neighbor girl, and even total strangers. You are the first one to buy a new purse but only because it also helps widows in Africa raise their children. This is so much like God, who loves to give good gifts to His children (Matthew 7:11). God's gifts are abundant, extravagant, and spilling over because He wants to delight His children.

You are also like God in that you exhibit the qualities of light. God is light (1 John 1:5) and Jesus called Himself the light of the world (John 8:12). What is light but pulsing energy? That's you! Just like your Father who lifts our moods with His divine voltage,

"The Lord upholds all who fall and lifts up all who are bowed down" (Psalm 145:14) and lightens our steps with His heavenly vigor, "He gives strength to the weary and increases the power of the weak" (Isaiah 40:29).

Doesn't it make you feel good to read about the many ways that you are like God? Doesn't it make you stand a little taller? Feel a bit more confident?

I sure hope it does.

God wants you to know of His loving intention behind your design, but He also needs you to be aware that your slice has an Achilles' heel, an area of weakness, that is vulnerable to a lie. This lie can remain dormant for years, rendering you clueless to its existence. But make no mistake; it is extremely dangerous. So dangerous that, if it's not weeded out, it can lead you astray and away from the One you reflect.

The Lie

Stephanie, a Connecter Mom of two and part-time hairstylist, has a cheerful, positive outlook on life. She's entertaining and engaging with everyone who sits in her chair at the salon where she works. She prides herself on her ability to connect with anyone—young or old, male or female, blonde or brunette—and on her ability to bring sunshine to their cloudy days. She believes that everyone should walk out of her salon with a great 'do and a better 'tude (or hair*do* and atti*tude* for those of you that don't speak Connecter). And they usually do.

But lately, she's been struggling with a family issue that is causing her deep concern. Her daughter, Haley, seems depressed. Haley is very gifted. She's an amazing artist, a talented musician, and an accomplished student, but she doesn't think she's good at anything. She is sullen and withdrawn and would rather spend time by herself in her room. She comes home from school, does her homework, practices the piano, then heads upstairs. She doesn't like large groups of people, so she won't sign up for youth group outings or talk to people at neighborhood parties.

Stephanie has tried to cheer her up with her usual jokes and funny stories, but she can't even get her to crack a smile. She's tried pointing out the good things in her life—their family, her friends, their church—but her encouragement falls on deaf ears. Stephanie doesn't want to wade too far into Haley's darkness for fear it will pull her under, so she keeps things light. She doesn't want to burden her friends and family with her struggle, so she keeps it all to herself. When sadness or disappointment rise up within her, she pushes those emotions down and tells herself to just be happy.

But Haley's mood is getting to Stephanie. It's eroding her confidence. She's starting to doubt her own worth.

Who is she if she can't connect with her own child?

Who is she if she can't infuse faith, hope, and love into her life?

Who is she if she can't inspire and energize?

Do you see the danger Stephanie is in? Do you see what happened? Somewhere along the way, Stephanie believed a lie, one that every Connecter must address at some point. The lie she believes is this: ***I am more valuable when I am making others happy.***

The problem is that Stephanie's *identity* has become tangled with her *personality*. She's confused her value with her gifting. Her worth became attached to the strengths of her slice rather than her place in the family of God.

Have you ever believed the lie?

On some level, haven't you felt that you are only as good as your good attitude? That you are more acceptable and lovable when you are celebrating, rejoicing, and spreading happiness to those around you? Haven't you felt that your value comes from pleasing others and making them happy? Do you assume that, when people are pleased with you, so is God? Haven't you wondered if God is disappointed in you when you're not happy?

Enough is enough. It's time to pull this lie out from the shadows, wrestle it to the ground, and send it to the pit of hell where it belongs. You are too precious to God to continue living this lie.

No matter what anyone says or how they respond to you, your value and your acceptability before God are not based on your ability to be everyone's sunshine. As Paul said, "If pleasing people were my goal, I would not be Christ's servant" (Galatians 1:10 NLT). Your value and acceptability before God are based on who you are—His daughter—*not* on what you do.

Yes, God gave you the strengths of the Connecter slice, but as Job pointed out, "The Lord gave and the Lord has taken away" (Job 1:21).

You can't get around it.

God prunes (John 15:2). He sometimes even cuts away the greatest assets in your life and renders them ineffective and seemingly useless, as He did in Stephanie's life, but during these times I believe He's doing the most significant work He'll ever do in your heart. You see, God must remove anything in which you've placed your confidence that is false or flimsy, even if that means rescinding the strengths of your slice. Anything that you love more than God, things that make you feel more acceptable, more presentable, more likable, or more loveable—must be dethroned. It's only when you are completely naked, stripped down to your most authentic self, and fully accepted in that state, that you will know that your value rests in His love and not in your strengths.

It hurts, this cutting away. And yet it is so necessary. He goes deep to lay a new foundation. He removes the old structures upon which you've instinctively built your worth and value (whether you knew you were doing that or not), and replaces the lie with an important truth. The truth is this: **Jesus delights in you *not* because you are happy but because you are *His*.**

The Journey to Truth

Once Stephanie realized that her value did not rest in cheering up her daughter, or anyone else, she was able to relax and hold her strengths lightly. She acknowledged that her strengths would allow her to serve others, but they didn't define her. God was the true source from which her gifts originated, so He could be in charge of lighting the way and enlivening the spirit.

Stephanie was still deeply concerned for her daughter's well-being, but once she stopped trying to save her with her strengths—in essence, trying to be her savior—she left room for her daughter to reach out to the real Savior. She prayed for Haley, supported her and loved her, but didn't make her daughter's happiness the measure of her own worth and value.

Stephanie learned that Jesus didn't need her to be happy. He wanted more for her than that—He wanted her to be filled with His joy. She admitted that, at times, she was forcing herself to be happy, trying hard to be cheerful and chipper. But joy is not something you manufacture; your joy, if it is to be real, comes from the Lord.

Where did she learn all this?

In solitude.

In time alone with God, with no one else around—a spiritual practice she had ignored for years due to her natural desire to be with others.

What she thought would feel like "solitary confinement" became the place of deepest connection her heart had ever known.

During these quiet times reading scripture and listening for God's voice, she discovered that true joy often has its roots in suffering. She saw it in the life of Jesus, a man of immeasurable joy, but also a "man of sorrows" (Isaiah 53:3 NLT). She understood it in Joseph's words when he named his son, Ephraim, which means "God has made me fruitful in the land of my suffering" (Genesis 41:52). Stephanie started to grasp that she would be more useful to God, not less, as she embraced, not minimized, her negative experiences and emotions. They didn't detract from her positivity, they deepened her joy.

The emotions she feared the most—darkness, depression, and maybe even despair—the ones she stuffed and hid, were the exact feelings she needed to expose in her times with God so that Jesus could turn her grief into joy (John 16:20).

And what often happens, as it did for Job, is that the Lord made Stephanie prosperous again. Not with Mega Millions, but with her slice. Her Connecter strengths, now God-infused, allowed her to sit with her daughter's sadness in a fresh way. She identified with her struggle as she admitted her own. She was able to offer her nourishing joy instead of sugary happiness. For the first time, Haley experienced God's presence through Stephanie's reflection of God and it inspired her to reach out to God herself.

Your Slice "on God"

If you would like to see what the Lord can do with your strengths, what your slice looks like "on God," you'll want to embrace the same spiritual practice as Stephanie.

Solitude.

Solitude is *the spiritual practice of separating from all people and activity with the clear intention of connecting with God.* Solitude includes times of silence to listen to God, but it can also include prayer, study of scripture, private worship, and journaling.

In solitude, you'll let go of your need for approval from others and find deep satisfaction in the approval of One.

In solitude, you'll be filled with God's love so you can love others from a Divine overflow.

In solitude, you will dive below the surface of frantic activity and discover deep spiritual treasures that are nestled in the heart and mind of God.

In solitude, your purpose in life becomes clear: to know yourself, to know Him, and to make Him known to others. If you're new to solitude, let me offer three practical tips that may help as you seek to establish your own habit of meeting with God:

1. Seek to listen rather than to speak. Words flow naturally from you as a running commentary on life. Sometimes it's hard to stop their flow and simply listen. But if you want to know what sweet things God might want to say to you, you'll have to pause and listen. First, declutter your mind by jotting down the thoughts that distract you. *I need to go to the post office. We're out of spaghetti sauce. I totally forgot; it's Teacher Appreciation Week.* Then set a timer on your phone for five minutes and ask God, "What do you want to say to me?" Breathe. Stay utterly still. God has been waiting to get your attention so He can talk to you. Give Him permission to speak anything, *anything,* to you. Say nothing. Just listen until your timer goes off.

2. Give God access to the full range of your emotions. Allow God to reveal aspects of your heart that may be invisible to you, or that you hide from, because they're troubled, sad, or even disgusting. There's nothing, *nothing* so awful in you that God can't handle. Lay everything bare before Him. Expose every ugly motive and selfish thought to His cleansing, healing light. As 1 John 1:7 says, "But if we walk in the light, as he is in the light, we have fellowship with one another, and the blood of Jesus, his Son, purifies us from all sin."

3. Fight for solitude. Create a daily meeting place for you to be with God. Candis's meeting place is her kitchen pantry. Tiff sits in her car in the garage. Kari's meeting spot is the bathroom, because with six kids, it's the only time she can be alone. Susannah Wesley, mother to Charles and John Wesley who founded the Methodist church, had nineteen children. How did she get time alone with God? She threw her apron up over her head in the middle of the kitchen, a sure sign no one was to disturb her. You can do this too (if you can find an apron!).

Certain seasons of motherhood lend themselves more easily to solitude than others, but one thing is true for every mother of every age: In our noisy, anti-God, anti-solitude world, you must fight daily for this space.

You may have avoided solitude in the past because the very word suggests loneliness and emptiness. And, as far as you know, people who practice solitude hum themselves into a deep trance while they ponder the meaning of life. Nothing about solitude sounds fun.

But this is the lie of Satan to keep you away from the presence of God.

Can I tell you something about the practice of solitude from my own experience? Solitude is not a dark and lonely place; it's a place of light and illumination. It's a place of wondrous self-discovery and of intimate connection with God. It's a place of beauty where I feel utterly safe and fully seen. Astonishing exchanges happen in this place that simply do not occur up on the surface. "Not only does the love of God come to us in solitude; the love of God begins to pour through us to others."[15]

Now, let your Father tell you how He feels about you and the beauty of your slice.

My **Connecter** Daughter,

From the moment you were conceived, I infused into your frame the knowledge that the world desperately needs joy. This is why you naturally insert fun and laughter into every event. Your sparkling smile and playful ways are meant to be contagious. In this world of pain, others may judge you as frivolous, but they miss the heart of you—that you desire to ease their load by bringing a smattering of hope and joy into their lives. You seek to be seen so you can offer this blessing to them.

I also wove into your DNA the knowledge that connection is vital for all human beings. You are part of My plan to join people together so they might see their need for one another. I love that you love others by connecting with them. As my Son said, to love others is the second greatest commandment. But remember that the first commandment is to love Me with all your heart, soul, mind, and strength.

I love to connect with you, not on a surface level, but on a deep level, where you allow my eyes to see every part of you. You are truly beautiful to Me and I take great delight in you. Will you put me on your calendar every day? Only as you daily grow in your love for Me can you truly love others with the kind of love they need. Please allow My Holy Spirit to play a vital role in your life. My Spirit gives you discernment about who you should connect with, and who you shouldn't, in any given moment. My Spirit provides the energy you need so you don't become depleted with all your giving to others.

Remember, you are not defined by your ability to shine and bring light. I am the Light of the World. It is only when My people follow Me, not you, that they escape darkness. Sometimes I bring sunshine and sometimes I bring rain. You work against Me if you encourage dancing and laughing during times I have ordained weeping and mourning. Do not fear suffering. Suffering is a gift. It is through the fellowship of suffering that my people experience communion with Me and experience firsthand the power of My resurrection. This is why you, too, must see suffering as a friend rather than an enemy.

I love you, Daughter. Look to Me, your True Mirror—not to others—to daily validate your worth because only I see you perfectly through the eyes of love.

With All My Love,
Your Father

CHAPTER 8

Improver: The "Quality Assurance" Mom

A thoughtful mom who uses her critical-thinking skills and beauti-ful mind to make everything better; a mom who corrects, refines, and teaches the difference between right and wrong, good and better.

Of the four mom types, you, dear Improver, are the most difficult to put into words because there is just so much to you. I scratch my head when I consider the wonderful nuances of you be-cause, in some ways, you defy explanation.

You're simply complicated. (Don't you love a good oxymoron?) A jumble of emotions and passions roil inside you, yet you display your-self to us as unruffled and straightforward. You like to be alone, and yet you desire meaningful connections with others. You're insightful and clever but often puzzled by your own complexity.

You're just different than other moms. According to the Institute for Motivational Living, only seven to twenty percent of the popula-tion shares your slice.

One quality I admire about you is your ability to absorb vast amounts of information. The inner architecture of your mind is able to comprehend and process words, thoughts, and ideas with unimaginable depth because your brain is a labyrinth of elaborate pathways and passages. You understand concepts the rest of us can't fathom. People often say to you, "That's brilliant. How did you think of that?" because you create new ways of doing things that blow our minds.

Psychologists, psychiatrists, and personality experts struggle to define you. Your personality type has been labeled "melancholy" (I'm sorry, it sounds so dark and depressing) and "analytical" (makes you sound more like a computer than a woman). One author even selected a beaver out of all the animals in the world to describe you. It's a giant rodent, for crying out loud.

Do you feel the limitations of these descriptors? I do. Because they miss the soul of who you are.

They miss what is at the core of your being, what drives you.

In a simple word, I think it's this: beauty.

You long for beauty—not the superficial beauty featured in magazines or catalogs—but beauty in its truest, most pure and perfected form. Ann Voskamp describes this pursuit in *One Thousand Gifts*:

> I want to see beauty. In the ugly, in the sink, in the suffering, in the daily, in all the days before I die, the moments before I sleep . . . This is what I crave: I hunger for beauty.[16]

Beauty calls to you because it connects you to your true self and to God, the author and perfecter of beauty. You feel one with God when you witness beauty, or are able to create a beauty that is, in your mind, both pure and perfect. Your design as an Improver is God's stamp of approval on the quest for beauty. When you seek it, you seek Him.

As you partner with God in your quest for beauty, you naturally seek to improve all things around you: yourself, your home, your garden, your children, even the family dog.

You may think, *Isn't this a driving factor for every mom?* No, not in the way it is for you. You must make something, or someone, better each and every day in order to feel good about yourself. This is part of your divine wiring.

Let's look at the unique way you help make your children better because of your special gifts and abilities.

Your Top Five Superpowers

While you may not be faster than a speeding bullet or more powerful than a locomotive, the conscientiousness that you apply to following the rules and the ways that you feel things deeply inspire admiration in the eyes of other moms.

As you read through your strengths, please take your time.

Let this list affirm you. Let it declare the beauty of your design.

But let this information also stir you. Use the questions at the end of each description to help you consider the ways you might use each superpower for even greater good in the lives of your children.

1. You're a mom with a plan. Unlike other moms who fly by the seat of their pants, everything that happens at your house has been carefully considered, organized, and prepared in advance. You're a logistical marvel. You've got a checklist for birthday parties, an itinerary for vacations, and a schedule for your day. Heading to the zoo? What if someone gets cold, hungry, or hurt? No worries, "readiness" is your middle name. Your purse is packed with snacks and in the back of your van are extra clothes and an emergency health kit—just in case.

In what ways does your ability to plan benefit your children?

2. You're a compassionate mom. You possess more heightened senses than the other three personality types, so you're able to look below surface responses to see the true emotions of your children, especially when they're in pain. You have a special tenderness for their nightmares, learning disorders, and struggles with social anxiety. You hurt when they hurt. You feel their pain when they lose a pet, a friend, or grandparent. You go deep into their sorrow and "suffer together" (the meaning of compassion) with them, so you can help carry their physical and emotional pain.

What suffering have you endured out of concern for your family?

3. You're a conscientious mom. Like the Marvel comic superheroes who fight evil and promote good, you spend your day making sure that good prevails. You model what is right and what is wrong in front of your kids, and you teach them the rules. *Elbows off the table. Respect your elders. Don't bite your friends.* If your children "miss the mark" in the manners and morals department, you correct them, and you do your best to model excellent habits to them on every level. You insist that your children tell the truth, keep their promises, and obey the law—just like you. You urge them to memorize verses, attend Sunday school every week, and participate in the family devotion at dinner because righteousness matters to you.

How have your principles improved your children's lives?

4. You're a mom who appreciates quality. Everything about you—how you work, what you create, and what you buy—is first-rate. You're selective. You have excellent taste and strong preferences. Organic cotton sheets and real wood toys for the baby. Top-ranked club teams and Newbery Medal readers for your middle-schooler. Premium field trips and vacations for the whole fam. It doesn't matter if you're camping in the woods or visiting the nation's capital, you want the moments to be remarkable. You're smart with money, knowing that, in the long run, cheap ends up costing more. Your silent mantra in all decisions is, "I want only the best for my family."

How do your high standards benefit your children?

5. You're a mom who values learning. You've got a focus on education. You read your children great works of literature and introduce them to classic films. You analyze the latest in smart toys and educational games, hoping to develop your children's brains in spatial reasoning, verbal memory, and fine motor skills. You urge your kids to sign up for the chess team, robotics club, or math olympics. Your passion for the arts exposes them to ballet, theater, and all kinds of museums. You encourage them to develop their own artistic abilities, and you urge them to master not just one instrument, but two.

How have you influenced your children's learning?

Look back over your superpowers. Do you see that the underlying motivation in all five is to teach your children high standards and help them be their best selves? What a blessing you are to them.

Follow the Leader

Katie is an Improver Mom with two boys.

During a coaching session, I asked her to give me a definition of an effective leader. She took a moment to think about her answer and then she articulated, "A leader is assertive and outgoing. She makes quick decisions. She knows what to do next and gets others to follow her without question."

"Who is your example of a good leader?" I asked.

"My mom. After dad died, she went back to work full time while raising me and my five brothers and sisters. She kept us all in line, especially the boys. And that's saying something. We all had assigned chores. We each did our part, no questions asked, no excuses accepted, because that's how mom operated. We secretly saluted her. We all admired her. And everything in our home ran like clockwork."

After she finished describing her mother, I asked, "Would you describe yourself as a leader?"

"No."

"Why not?"

"Because I'm not like my mom. I'm careful. I take my time and don't move until I am sure. I can't even decide on a new toothpaste for the kids until I research it and consult three dentists. I'm cautious and not as decisive as my mom. I over-think every decision, which sometimes paralyzes me."

"Do you realize that you just described another way to lead? You're known as a deliberate leader, one who decides and acts consciously and intentionally," I responded.

Katie looked at me skeptically, as if she wasn't sure that this was a valid style of leadership. It took a bit more explanation for her to fully understand her unique leadership style, but once she did, she became more confident in leading her family according to her special slice.

Let's look at the type of leader you are as an Improver Mom.

You're a respected leader. You have what pastor and author Andy Stanley refers to as "moral authority." Moral authority, he says, is "the credibility you earn by walking your talk. It is the relationship other people see between what you say and what you do, between what you claim to be and what you are."[17] Your yes is yes, your no is no. When you drop off and pick up your children, you're on time. When you sign up for a dish, a donation, or a volunteer role, you follow through on your commitment. When you set a limit, you hold the line. You are a great coach for any sport and an esteemed leader for any scouting troop because you know the rules and abide by the terms of the organization.

You're a vigilant leader. From the industrial baby latches to the 130 SPF sunscreen, you are committed to protecting your children from danger. There's nothing to fear when mom is near. You don't let them waste their allowance, get near strangers, or share their address on social media. You make sure they wash their hands, use their sanitizer, and keep their shoes by the front door. Your passion for safety will guard their hearts, souls, minds, and bodies for years to come and keep them from burning down the house.

You're a detailed leader. Emily Dickinson said, "If you take care of the small things, the big things take care of themselves."[18] This is your leadership motto. Your kids feel seen, noticed, and important (significant stuff in the life of a child), all because you attend to what others consider small. For example, you pay attention to the love languages of your children, providing words of affirmation to one and quality time to another. You know your son likes to wear his favorite athletic leggings on Monday, so you have them clean by Sunday evening. When your daughter casually requests Pink Knickers nail polish or extra pencils for school, you buy them and put them in her room.

You're a knowledgeable leader. Before making a decision, you do your homework. Before your baby was born, you'd already researched the best crib, family photographer, and essential oils. These days, you listen to podcasts and study parenting books. You read mom blogs. You're the expert on most any subject. Your children trust your choices. Moms from far and wide solicit your advice because it's always based on meticulous thought and thorough investigation.

You're a leader with conviction. You feel compassion for human suffering, so you throw your support behind projects that feed the hungry and heal the sick. You expose your children to the injustices in the world—poverty, inequality, and human trafficking—and show them how they can make a difference. The funds received through lemonade stands, bake sales, and allowances are put to good use improving the quality of life for those around the globe and seeking fair and impartial treatment for all.

It's true! You are amazing with your five distinctive superpowers and your unique style of leadership. But that doesn't ensure that bullets will bounce off your chest! Yes, you *are* a super mom, but, like all of us, you have your vulnerabilities. Let's consider these now.

Improver Mom Kryptonite

All superheroes come with inherent weaknesses. Sad but true. (Unless, of course, you are Wonder Woman, who is an anomaly even in the superhero world.) Case in point: Daredevil. His heightened senses allow him to sniff out even the faintest whiff of an enemy, but if he's bombarded with an excessive amount of odor, he's paralyzed and useless. His humanity makes him susceptible to injury and illness. And oh yeah, he's blind. And you, Super Improver Mom, with your slice of God's image, have your own vulnerabilities, too.

You already know some of these because you constantly wrestle with them in your mind. You don't like to think about your weaknesses because they make you feel unsafe. Unprotected. Vulnerable.

As author Brene Brown says in *Daring Greatly,* "Vulnerability looks like courage in you, but feels like inadequacy in me."[19] When you confess where you are weak, we see bravery, not failure. We move closer to you, feeling a deep appreciation for your authentic soul and wanting to connect with you in a significant way. We admire your honesty and respect you even more.

As difficult as it may seem, I ask you to embrace these weaknesses. Remember, we all have shortcomings, but I promise you, they can become your ticket to a greater connection with others and a greater connection with God.

I've put these weaknesses in the form of questions because, more than likely, these are the questions you ask yourself when you're ensnared in a weakness.

Why am I so hard on myself and others? Because you yearn for beauty in its purest and most perfect form, you tend to set the bar a tad too high. This tendency toward perfectionism produces high-quality results but takes its toll on your relationships. You never feel good enough and neither do your kids. They make a minor mistake and they feel you treat it like a first-degree felony. They act their age and you criticize them for immature behavior. They clean their entire room and you point out the one dirty sock under the bed.

As a new Airbnb host, I got a little nervous when Improvers stayed with me. Those high standards are intimidating. One Improver guest was *very* disappointed in the cleanliness of the kitchen. After three hours of cleaning on my part, she said there was a "thick layer of grunge" on the microwave. As a mom of four children, I know grunge. I know sticky and icky, and there was no grunge on that oven. To alleviate her concern, I immediately started wiping it down, trying to find all that grunge, while she went to retrieve the cleaning wipes she had brought with her on vacation.

No one is perfect. We all miss the mark. "For all have sinned and fall short of the glory of God" (Romans 3:23). So give yourself and others a break. When critiquing your child's work, praise the good. Ask if they want your feedback. If the answer is no, hold your tongue. If the answer is yes, share just a couple of things. If you compliment your child, put a period on it. Don't follow it up with a "but . . ." Start a gratitude journal. Accept a little grunge in life—it builds character, your immune system, and as my mom says, "puts hair on your chest." That's supposed to be a good thing.

Why do I overthink everything? Because your brain is wired to process large amounts of information, it's easy for you to ruminate endlessly on the "what ifs" of an issue. *What if this is the wrong paint color? What if I say the wrong thing? What if going back to work is a bad decision?* This state of analysis paralysis makes you feel overwhelmed, stressed, and chronically tired. At night, while everyone else is asleep, you're awake because you can't find the "off" switch for your brain.

Philippians 4:6 says, "Do not be anxious about anything, but in every situation, by prayer and petition, with thanksgiving, present your requests to God."

Instead of talking to yourself about an issue, talk to God. Ask for wisdom. He gives it generously without finding fault (James 1:5).

Set a "drop-dead" date to act. Share your thoughts with a friend you trust to help you detangle your options and prioritize your goals. On a regular basis, ask God to show you when you are about to cross the line from healthy evaluation into toxic over-thinking.

Why is my glass half-empty? Because your eagle eye can spot problems before others, you tend to focus on what's *wrong* rather than what's *right*. You notice your daughter's one B instead of the five As. You beat yourself up over the errands that didn't get done, instead of celebrating what you did finish. And you worry constantly that, according to Murphy's Law, what can go wrong, will.

You may call yourself a realist, but scientific studies show that a pessimistic outlook lowers your immunity, causes you to give up more easily, and feel depressed more often.[20] Heightened negative emotions have also been linked to an overactive amygdala and a decrease in serotonin activity, the happiness hormone.[21]

Psalm 43:5 says, "Why, my soul, are you downcast? Why so disturbed within me? Put your hope in God, for I will yet praise him, my Savior and my God."

Open up to optimism, the belief that God has good in store for you and, with His help, all things are possible. Also, include a positive observation with every "improvement" you offer. Voicing the good in the situation first will balance your constructive criticism and help you overcome your natural tendency toward pessimism.

Why is forgiveness so hard for me? Because justice is central to your nature, you struggle to forgive. Forgiveness often seems illogical. You think: *I can't let little Wyatt off the hook. He deserves punishment for what he did.* Or, *What Alexa did was indisputably wrong. If I forgive her, aren't I saying that what she did was okay?* You rank sin, believing the offenses of others to be worse than your own, which provides justification for blame.

Forgiving is *not* excusing or condoning bad behavior. True forgiveness simply places the responsibility for justice into God's hands. Think of forgiveness as a transfer of ownership. Instead of holding onto the injustice yourself, hand it over to God. Let Him be responsible for it. Release your hurt, your pain, and the wrong that was done to you into His capable hands. God loves justice. He's actually the author of justice, so He will act fairly and rightly with the offense in His perfect time.

Ephesians 4:32 perfectly summarizes what our attitude should be: "Be kind and compassionate to one another, forgiving each other, just as in Christ God forgave you."

Why am I so black and white? Of the four personality types, you spend more time working out of the left side of your brain, which is the place of logic. You think about something and come to a logical conclusion about how to do it that is, in your mind, the "right way." You hang your toilet paper the right way. (For the rest of us, over is right, under is wrong.) You fold your towel the right way. (In thirds, lengthwise.) You burp your baby, set the table, and of course, load your dishwasher the right way (everyone else can look these things up on the internet).

Because you firmly establish what is good and bad—because you've researched it and it makes sense—you don't leave room for other methods. Your opinions quickly turn to facts and you judge alternative ways as misguided and mistaken.

Ecclesiastes 3:1 says, "There is a time for everything, and a season for every activity under the heavens."

Embrace difference. The way your husband makes the bed might not be the most efficient approach, or even qualify as a best practice, but that doesn't make it wrong. See your way as a preference based on your precise Improver nature, and come to understand the motivation of each Authentic Personality Type. If they're Doers, they go for speed. If they're Connecters, they seek fun. If they're Stabilizers, they keep things peaceful.

What's My Trigger?

Every mom has a trigger, a button that, when pushed, can morph her into "scary mommy." The trigger for each personality type is different, but some of the emotions that emerge are similar.

You feel it welling up. Embarrassment. Insecurity. Anxiety.

You're worried that you could blow. You don't want it to happen, but sometimes it does. You scream. You shame. You sink into a dark, melancholy state.

You wonder if there's something wrong with you.

No, nothing is wrong with you.

Then what? What's the cause of this mommy meltdown?

Let me tell you straight up.

The thing that triggers you is **criticism.**

When your children complain about the dinner you painstakingly prepared or your boss finds a mistake in the spreadsheet you carefully compiled, you take it personally. When your mother questions your method of discipline or choice of school (which took you fifteen months to decide), you feel judged. When you're forced into a deadline that causes you to compromise your standards, you feel triggered.

Criticism, the act of finding fault, stings you more than anyone else because your heart's desire is to make things better, to improve everything that you touch. It makes sense. Your critical eye and your keen mind have been designed for accuracy, so you feel diminished when you can't deliver.

You hate it when others criticize you, but let's be real here.

Your biggest critic is you.

You are more critical of yourself than anyone could ever be of you.

When you forget to buy milk, you call yourself "stupid." When you gaze at that extra ten pounds of baby weight, you say to yourself: "ugly." Throughout your day, you tell yourself, "too much." "not enough." "weird."

Sound familiar?

You'd never in a million years speak words like that to your kids or your friends, but when it comes to you, you can't seem to help yourself.

So how do you silence your inner critic?

Become aware. These inner critic voices are usually so familiar that they exist under your intellectual radar, wreaking havoc without your awareness.

So call them out.

Look at them in the light of day.

Ask yourself, and those closest to you, three simple questions. Is the statement true? Is it helpful? Does it deserve the mental real estate that you've given it?

If the answer is no, and it usually is 99.999 percent of the time, then ask God: *What do You want to say to me?*

He will probably start by telling you that He loves you just as you are, warts and all. I like to picture myself wearing one of those "As Is" stickers that you find on the broken items in the clearance section. It reminds me that God bought me just as I am. He was warned about my condition and He made the purchase anyway. And no matter what the return policy, He's promised to never take me back.

He feels the same way about you, dear sister. He finds you to be adorable with your "As Is" sticker, too.

I love this quote from Tim Keller because it describes our humble and noble authentic selves: "We are more sinful and flawed in ourselves than we ever dared believe, yet at the very same time we are more loved and accepted in Jesus Christ than we ever dared hope."[22]

Self-Compassion

One of the best ways to protect yourself from being triggered in the first place is to practice ongoing self-compassion.

God has compassion for you (Psalm 103:8). So it's okay to be kind to yourself, as God is kind toward you.

Here are five things you can do for yourself that will refill, refuel, and refresh you as an Improver Mom.

Dig deep into God's Word. Improvers connect to God most naturally through His written word, the Bible. And because you thrive with routine and have a thirst to know more, you need a regular appointment with God where you have time to search the Bible and read it in detail. A short daily devotion isn't going to do it for you. You need time each day to ask the hard questions, explore different schools of thought, and understand the deep and hidden things of God.

Join a Bible study at church or choose a study for yourself. Get a Bible in One Year app for your phone. With your discipline and intentionality, you're one of the few moms who can actually pull that off—something we all admire.

Go to your room! This is a biggie. Due to your introverted nature and tendency toward overstimulation, it's imperative that you have alone time every single day. No, you're not antisocial. You simply need to be by yourself to process and reflect, to contemplate, and to order the thoughts and ideas from the day. Sit on your porch and enjoy the spaciousness of the outdoors. Work in the yard. Do yoga on your mat. Journal. If there's no way to be alone (because, ahem, you are a mom), close your eyes for as long as you can, preferably not while driving.

Clean like it's spring. You function best mentally and emotionally when your house is tidy, the files are alphabetized, and everything is in its place. Order fills your emotional cup. So pick one project you can finish in the amount of time you have (because completion also floats your boat). Reorganize your son's closet. Group the kids' books by reading level. Clean out the car and polish the steering wheel (you know you want to). As it says in 1 Thessalonians 4:7, "God hasn't invited us into a disorderly, unkempt life but into something holy and beautiful—as beautiful on the inside as the outside" (MSG). Let your one act of organizing stamp a smile on your heart because you cooperated with God in bringing order to the world.

Get lost in a sunset. Nothing refreshes you like taking in beauty. Treat your eyes, ears, nose, hands, and taste buds to something exquisite. Take a walk with your kids after dinner and allow the majesty of a sunset to envelop you. Plan a "me" morning on Saturday to stroll through the museum of contemporary art. Plug into *Phantom of the Opera* on your earbuds while you're mopping the floor or driving to work. Read poetry before you go to bed. Plant lavender in your garden. Eat something decadent, filled with warm caramel and drizzled with dark chocolate.

Take in beauty, but also express it through your God-given creativity. When you create, you get out of the left side of your brain (the logic side) and enter into the right side (the creative side) where your thoughts can free-flow. Write a poem or a song. Break out the watercolors. Practice the piano. Take beautiful photos of your children. As Joseph Chilton Pearce says, "We must accept that this creative pulse within us is God's creative pulse itself."[23] What could refresh you more than allowing God's spirit to flow through you as you create something beautiful?

Have coffee with a friend that "gets" you. You don't need the whole world to understand you, but you do need a few empathetic soulmates who notice when you're unhappy or scared, and can feel what you feel. You need someone to listen, to draw you out, and to ask questions that help you go beyond surface talk.

Pursue relationships with those who can go deep. Extroverts like quantity, but you need quality. Skip the group events and schedule one-on-one time with a friend. If you have deeper hurts (and who doesn't?), pursue counseling or find a mentor who can be trusted with your confessions. Two women in my life, one a mentor and one a therapist, met this need for me in a significant way when my disclosures were a little too heavy for the average mom to bear.

Remember, not everyone is like you. If your best friend and husband are different personality types, they may not have your same needs for sensitivity, solitude, or order. Don't let that deter you. Acknowledge your needs and take care of them. Steward yourself and the superpowers you have to share. Your family will thank you for it.

The next chapter will take this a step further. You'll learn how your design as an Improver Mom mirrors God and what you have been gifted to reflect. You'll also learn how to overcome the lie that you're most likely to believe about yourself and how God wants to inhabit your slice and infuse it with His divinity.

CHAPTER 9

Discover God's Design for Improvers

Your past is waiting to inspire you.

At least that's what Ancestry.com says.

You've probably seen the commercials. An exotic beauty is curious about her heritage. She's always believed that her peeps are from Africa, but knows nothing beyond that. She takes the test and gets her results. She's not at all who she thought she was. Turns out she's twenty-four percent Native American, twenty-two percent Irish, seventeen percent African, sixteen percent Italian, twelve percent Asian, and the list goes on. Now that's what I call diversity! Go ahead, do the math, Improver Moms (which you've probably already done because you've got a head for numbers).

She's excited because now she knows where she got her sculpted cheekbones and her almond-shaped eyes. She feels like she has a whole new family and wonders what they've passed on to her.

Genealogy, the study of your personal heritage, can tell you about the people and the places that God has used to bring you into this world and, honestly, it's quite fascinating. But it can't tell you about your spiritual heritage, the inheritance you've received from your heavenly Father.

This is where your personality slice becomes important.

Your slice is His stamp of approval imprinted on who you are and who He made you to be. It's a visible declaration of His favor toward you. He likes who you are. He made you this way.

When God looks at you, He smiles because you remind Him of Himself. Let me tell you how.

Your Inheritance

Like you, God loves order. His creation is built on systematic order. First, God brought light. Next, He created the sky. After that, He made the land and the seas. He continued in this methodical pattern, sequentially adding trees, stars, and animals before creating His crowning glory: man and woman. When He placed Adam and Eve in the Garden, he told them to work the land and "keep it in order" (Genesis 2:15 MSG). Don't you love how you share your organizational skills with Him?

Like you, God loves truth and justice. His Word is true. His law is true. His commands are true. As the Trinity—Father, Son, and Spirit—He is the one true God. Jesus described Himself as the way, the *truth*, and the life (John 14:6, italics mine). He is the true vine and the true light. Truth is intrinsic to His nature. Psalm 45:4 prophecies that Jesus, in His majesty will "ride forth victoriously in the cause of truth, humility and justice" as a rider who is Faithful and True (Revelation 19:11).

Like you, God is a planner. His words to the prophet Jeremiah on behalf of the exiled Israelites have always brought me comfort and peace. "'For I know the plans I have for you,' declares the Lord, 'plans to prosper you and not to harm you, plans to give you hope and a future'" (Jeremiah 29:11). You just can't beat that.

When Adam and Eve unleashed sin into the world through their disobedience, all seemed lost on a human level, but God already had a plan in mind. God said to Satan, "I will put enmity between you and the woman, and between your offspring and hers; he will crush your head, and you will strike his heel" (Genesis 3:15). God was speaking of a future day when Satan would strike at Jesus during His life on earth, but Christ would crush and defeat him when He rose from the dead. God's plan, from the beginning of time, has always been to make payment for our sin (and redeem the lost) so that we might live.

Like you, God delights in the details. Were you aware that up to one *million* animal species live in the world's oceans? And it's believed that another one-third to two-thirds have yet to be named and described.[24] Did you know that experts in astrophysics have predicted that there are about 100 *million* stars in the average galaxy and there are now thought to be two *trillion* galaxies in the universe?[25] Isn't that crazy? From the depths of the ocean to the expanses beyond the sky, we can see that the ability to create extensive variety requires a divine eye for microscopic detail. God is clearly captivated by details. He wields them to produce this wondrously complex and diverse world that we call home.

Like you, God is compassionate to those who are hurting. In Exodus 22:27, He says it plainly, "When they cry out to me, I will hear, for I am compassionate." God's compassion allowed Israel to be shown compassion by their captor (2 Chronicles 30:9). His tender mercy sent deliverers to rescue His people (Nehemiah 9:27). And because of His extravagant compassion, God has blotted out all our transgressions (Psalm 51:1).

Like you, God values quality. When instructing the Israelites in the offerings they were to bring Him, God told them to bring the best of the first fruits. Similar to what He will bring us at the end of the age: "On this mountain the Lord Almighty will prepare a feast of rich food for all peoples, a banquet of aged wine—the best of meats and the finest of wines" (Isaiah 25:6). God wants us to pursue excellence. He wants us to push beyond average and ordinary. After all, He is no ordinary God. He wants us to think about things that are excellent (Philippians 4:8), discern what is best (Philippians 1:10), and concentrate on doing our best for God (2 Timothy 2:15 MSG).

Just like you, God loves beauty. When He planted the Garden of Eden, He included "trees that were pleasing to the eye" (Genesis 2:9) as well as those that were good for food. He didn't just create things that were useful, He created things that were beautiful, too. "He has made everything beautiful in its time" (Ecclesiastes 3:11). One aspect of God's glory is His beauty. "Perfect in beauty, God shines forth" (Psalm 50:2). In the Old Testament, we learn that "the heavens declare the glory of God" (Psalm 19:1). The sun, sky, and stars display His beauty. In the New Testament, we see God's beauty displayed through Jesus Christ. "The son is the radiance of God's glory" (Hebrews 1:3). What is more beautiful than that?

Doesn't it make you feel good to read about the many ways you are like God? Doesn't it make you stand a little taller? Feel a bit more confident? I sure hope it does.

God wants you to know of His loving intention behind your design, but He also needs you to be aware that your slice has an Achilles' heel, an area of weakness, that is vulnerable to a lie. This lie can remain dormant for years, rendering you clueless to its existence. But make no mistake. It is extremely dangerous. So dangerous that, if it's not weeded out, it can lead you astray and away from the One you reflect.

The Lie

Emily is an Improver Mom to three biological children and one adopted child from Ethiopia. In the early years of their marriage, Emily and her husband served as missionaries in Africa. They witnessed firsthand the poverty of the region, and it broke their hearts. The plight of orphans consumed their thoughts. After many years of consideration and prayer, they started the adoption process. Emily was diligent with the paperwork and thoroughly prepared for home study visits. She researched every topic they would need to know about—from biracial families and Ethiopian culture to child development and broken family attachments. They waited patiently, respecting the procedures and protocols of international adoption, until finally the day came when they flew across the globe and brought home their little boy. They were certain that God had hand-picked Abel for their family.

That was seven years ago. Abel is now thirteen. Emily didn't expect that bringing another child into their home would be easy, but she never dreamed it would come to this.

"Abel is angry, in a dangerous way," Emily said during our coaching session. "Abel's been in trouble at home, at school, and even with the police."

Some of his behavioral problems could be linked to recent diagnoses by medical doctors, teachers who identified learning disabilities, and a psychiatrist who said Abel had oppositional defiant disorder (ODD).

"Dale, I've tried everything. I put in place family rules so he had structure and boundaries. I disciplined him with love and created a safe home for him. We all worked together to affirm and accept him. But Abel has pushed us all away."

Emily's voice cracked. "I feel like such a failure. I'm so sad that I can't even go out in public anymore. I can't tell anyone what's going on because it's too embarrassing. My other three children tell me constantly, 'Abel gets away with everything. It's not fair.' And now they are acting out, too."

Then she admits the secret regret she's never spoken out loud to anyone. "Sometimes I almost wish we'd never brought him into our home."

Emily is in crisis. It's not just her family's well-being that's on the line; it's her identity as a mom.

Who is she if she can't bring discipline and order to their home?

Who is she if her kids keep making endless mistakes and poor choices?

Who is she if she has lost compassion for her own child?

Do you see what has happened? Somewhere along the way, Emily believed a lie, one that every Improver must address at some point. The lie she believes is this: *I am more valuable when I produce a perfect result.*

Here's the problem. Emily's *identity* has become tangled with her *personality*. She is confusing her value with her gifting. Her worth has become attached to the strengths of her slice rather than her place in the family of God.

Have you ever believed the lie?

On some level, haven't you felt like God was disappointed in you when you failed, and that He was withholding His acceptance until you got it right? Haven't you imagined God's voice accusing you of your sins and replaying them over and over until you were able to achieve a perfect result? Haven't you felt unlovable or unacceptable when you failed to meet His holy standards? Haven't you worked yourself silly to prove you could do better?

Enough is enough. It's time to pull this lie out from the shadows, wrestle it to the ground, and send it to the pit of hell where it belongs. You are too precious to God to continue living this lie.

The truth is this: God accepts you just as you are (Romans 15:7).

Let me say that again, because this truth needs to take root, not just in your head, but also in your heart. God accepts you as you are—even in your messy, sinful, weak, and imperfect state.

I know it's hard to believe, but it's true. God exchanged your imperfect sin nature for Christ's perfect righteousness (2 Corinthians 5:21). He doesn't need your perfection to accomplish His perfect will even in the lives of your children. Your worth, which is established by Christ, is priceless—in your current imperfect state.

Yes, God gave you the strengths of the Improver slice—excellence, order, justice—but as Job pointed out, "The Lord gave and the Lord has taken away" (Job 1:21).

You can't get around it.

God prunes (John 15:2). He sometimes even cuts away the greatest assets in your life and renders them ineffective and seemingly useless, as He did in Emily's life, but during these times, I believe He's doing the most significant work He'll ever do in your heart. You see, God must remove anything in which you've placed your confidence that is false or flimsy, even if that means rescinding the strengths of your slice. Anything that you love more than God, things that make you feel more acceptable, more presentable, more likable, or more loveable—must be dethroned. It's only when you are completely naked, stripped down to your most raw self, and fully accepted in that state, that you will know that your value rests in His love and not in your strengths.

It hurts, this cutting away. And yet it is so necessary. God goes deep to lay a new foundation. He removes the old structures upon which you've instinctively built your worth and value (whether you knew you were doing that or not), and replaces your lie with an important truth. The truth is this: **Jesus delights in you *not* because you are perfect but because you are *His*.**

The Journey to Truth

Emily acknowledged that she was a bit of a perfectionist, but it wasn't until her Bible study group took a closer look at Satan in the book of Ezekiel that she began to see the danger of this attitude. She had known that Satan was an angel, the highest ranking being that God had created, but she had not realized that the Bible describes him as "the *model of perfection*, full of wisdom and *perfect in beauty*" (Ezekiel 28:12, italics mine). Satan was stunningly beautiful, breathtakingly perfect, full of light and glory. But his strengths were his ruin. Pride entered Satan's heart.

Satan's perfection made him proud. Pride was his downfall, and it could have been Emily's, too, if she hadn't taken a different approach and humbled herself.

She wrote out a prayer to God.

Father, please forgive me for my arrogance. You know that I only wanted to uphold your standards, respect your ways, and obey your laws. I've desperately wanted that for my family, too. But my need to "do things right" has made me proud. I thought that my good behavior pleased you, so I elevated my performance over my heart. I preferred perfection to reality, at times trying harder to look good rather than be good. I was wrong. No one is good but You alone.

Next, Emily came out of hiding and got honest with her friends. She told them about Abel's behavior and his trouble with the police. She feared that they would think she had no standards and that she was soft on truth, so she watched their reactions for any signs of judgment. But, instead, they nodded their heads in understanding and shed empathetic tears on her behalf. They welcomed her humility and applauded her vulnerability. They said they felt closer to her than ever before. And although she admittedly looked like a worse mother, because she was now coming clean with her problems, she gained deeper friendships. This was a healing step for her.

Emily learned that true improvement is a messy process. To look more like Christ, from the inside out, to truly reflect His holiness and perfection, took courage and work. It meant admitting her weaknesses and trusting God to be her strength. It meant accepting the fact that Jesus didn't need her to be perfect. He wanted more for her than that—He wanted her to be real, to need Him, to stop trying to bring holiness on her own.

She also discovered that there was another way to look at beauty, best described by Shauna Niequist, in her book *Present Over Perfect*:

"I find myself drawn to mess, to darkness, to things that are loved to the point of shabbiness, or just wildly imperfect in their own gorgeous way."[26]

It was a novel thought that real, more than perfection, was beautiful to God, but one that her heart was ready to embrace. She made being real rather than being "right" her goal.

As Emily realized that her value did not rest in being perfect, she was able to relax and hold her strengths lightly. She acknowledged that her strengths would allow her to serve her family, but they didn't define her. God was the true source from which her gifts originated, so He could be in charge of making things right and bringing excellence to her family.

And that is exactly what happened. Her Improver strengths, now God-infused, allowed her to accept her son's issues in a fresh way. She identified with his struggles as she admitted her own. She was able to offer him loving excellence instead of impossible perfection. She continued to hold the line with Abel, while God worked in his heart, in His timing, in His way.

Your Slice "on God"

Do you want to see what your slice looks like "on God?" Then follow Emily's example.

Practice humility.

Humility is not a *woe is me* attitude, but a *low is me* perspective. It's a willingness to be like Christ, who "did not consider equality with God something to be used to his own advantage; rather, he made himself nothing" (Philippians 2:6–7). It is an ongoing acknowledgment that God is above you, His ways are higher than your own, and you bow before Him as the blessed controller of all things.

When you practice humility, you empty yourself regularly. You let go of your own righteousness and goodness so that you can embrace God's righteousness and goodness on your behalf.

When you practice humility, you find solace from the constant need to perform and to pretend that you have it all together.

When you practice humility, you find connection with others, as fellow sojourners on the journey of sanctification.

When you practice humility, you find the improvement you seek. You cannot act like Christ on your own; you need God's presence and authority in your life to be changed.

If you're new to humility, let me offer three practical tips that may help you establish this daily practice:

1. Make being real your goal. God knows that you are weak and prone to sin (even as an Improver) and, unlike the Pharisees, the respectable church leaders of Jesus' day, He wants you to be real about it. The Pharisees refused to be real with Jesus and He condemned them for it. "Woe to you, teachers of the law and Pharisees, you hypocrites! You clean the outside of the cup and dish, but inside they are full of greed and self-indulgence" (Matthew 23:25).

Real is an inside job. Focus on what's going on in your mind and your heart before you consider your outside behavior. Notice your attitudes, your thoughts, and your innermost feelings. This is where Jesus wants to work with you. If you entrust yourself to the Holy Spirit, He will work in you, and that will eventually show up on the outside.

2. *Veto the lies.* Satan always tells you that you must do better, be better, and think better in order to be acceptable. Remember, Satan is your accuser, "the father of lies" (John 8:44). He wants to turn your practice of humility into a state of humiliation, so you give up and go home. Please don't let him.

When the thought comes, "I'm stupid," or "I'm a failure," or "I'm not good enough," pause that thought on the screen of your mind and call it what it is: a lie, an accusation, from the enemy of God. Tell Satan that he has no place in your mind and order him to leave. "Resist the devil, and he will flee from you" (James 4:7). Then speak the truth out loud: "I am loved by God, I am His child, and I am acceptable just as I am." Lies and accusations (which are vastly different from the gentle voice of God's correction) are toxic to that beautiful mind of yours, so train your mind to silence Satan's lies.

3. *Share with others.* James 5:16 urges, "Confess your sins to each other and pray for each other so that you may be healed." Counteract your sense of superiority by sharing your failures, sins, or fears with another person.

I know. The thought of telling someone your shortcomings sounds terrifying, risky. Yes, you risk rejection, judgment, or being misunderstood. You risk looking foolish or weak. So why confess? Because confession humbles you and protects you from arrogance. And if you don't confess, you might miss out on the greatest blessing of all—someone who sees your failure, embraces you with open arms, and says, "Me, too." Or, "I love you, flaws and all."

Of course, be wise about the person you select to hear your heart. The authors of *Safe People* tell us to avoid confessing to a critic. Critics are more concerned with confronting errors than making connection. Critics are quick to point the finger at others, rather than at themselves. Critics love truth but devalue relationship.[27]

For me, being humble requires intentionality and awareness, but it is certainly not the degrading condition I assumed it would be. While hard at first, like new things always are, it turned out to be a soft place to land. At first, when I let my authentic self be known by admitting what was going on in my life, I felt like I would fall *from* grace, but what I found was that I fell *into* grace.

Humility taught me about the extravagance of grace, the soft side of God's love. Humility was the door that ushered me into a deep understanding of my identity in Christ—broken and beloved. Humility allowed me to see my Father's loving nature and receive His unconditional acceptance. I never knew I could be accepted in my imperfect state until I revealed my imperfect state, and He was right there to welcome me. Humility has helped me surrender to God's pleasing and perfect will, knowing that He is good and can be trusted in every way. Humility has changed my life.

I'll conclude this chapter with one of my favorite verses, James 4:6: "God opposes the proud but gives grace to the humble" (NLT).

Grace is for the humble. Grace is for those who are real. Grace is for those who surrender themselves to the living God.

You can't get it any other way.

Now, let your Father tell you how He feels about you and the beauty of your slice.

My **Improver** Daughter,

Do you know how much I love you? Do you understand how delighted I am that you aspire to beauty and excellence, that you constantly look for ways to improve your home, your community, and the world around you? I have given you a creative mind that is able to see beauty and potential greatness in all things. This is why you pursue excellence in all you think and do.

I gifted you with a tender heart, one that is sensitive to what breaks My own heart. You shed tears for the struggles and suffering of My people. You feel things deeply. These strong emotions create solid convictions in your life. You fight for justice and you strive to right the wrongs of life. Like Me, you are willing to make great sacrifices on behalf of others and on behalf of worthy causes.

I created you with a dynamic brain that can process much information on multiple levels. You have an eye for the smallest detail and the ability to carefully assess the complexities of a situation, identify risks, and create a safe and solid pathway to follow. People often come to you for answers because they see your abilities as a creative, critical thinker.

Your thirst for knowledge and your desire to learn are beautiful in My sight, but be careful. If you pursue knowledge for knowledge's sake, you will become arrogant because knowledge "puffs up." Train your mind to seek Me. Remember, while your inquisitive mind is strong and able, it is limited. Your thoughts are not My thoughts. I have given you the mind of Christ, but you must stay close to Me if you are to know My thoughts and demonstrate My principles in a world that desperately needs My love.

You work endlessly to think and do the right things. This pleases Me. But there is something you do that saddens My heart. When you fail to live up to the high standards you set for yourself, you berate yourself and call yourself hateful names. This causes Me pain. You are my treasure, my prized possession. Be kind to yourself. If you need correction, come to Me, and I will gently instruct you. Let go of your need to be perfect. I see you through the beauty and perfection of my Son Jesus, who died for you. You can never be more perfect to Me than you are right now. What I desire is simply that you act justly, love mercy, and walk humbly with Me.

With All My Love,
Your Father

CHAPTER **10**

Doer: The "Get 'Er Done" Mom

A zoom-zoom mom who is quick to act, quick to solve problems, and quick to take on responsibility.

When I was pregnant with my first child, I found myself sitting next to a famous gospel singer on a business flight to Orlando. He had been bumped from first class and God plopped him down on the other side of the veil, in coach, next to me.

We chatted on and off throughout the flight and then, as the plane prepared to land, he turned to me and said, "I have a word from the Lord for you." I sat tall. Wow. That sounded big. Important. And slightly scary. (I hoped he wouldn't be using the word "smite.")

He looked intently into my eyes and, in his booming baritone voice declared, "Bold. Be bold." Then he put his tray table up, buckled his seat belt, and looked out the window.

That's it? No more words from the Lord? No specifics about what He meant?

Before we deplaned and went our separate ways, I smiled politely and thanked him for the word. But I wondered, Be bold how? Be bold where? Be bold when?

Looking back on that moment, I'm glad the message from God was simple. Bold. I love that word. It's large and big. Bold fits everything I do. It's a word that validates who I am as a Doer.

It's not easy being a Doer, especially as a woman. Our type is strong and powerful, descriptors that seem more masculine than feminine. We are gutsy and fierce, ready to fight for those we love. We leap into action and tackle projects with a tenacity that leaves others scratching their heads and questioning the level of our caffeine intake.

Doers are a bit of a rarity. The Institute for Motivational Living reports that only about three to ten percent of people share our personality type.

I've also come to believe that my word from the Lord is also your word. So please hear me as I say to you, "Be bold, dear Doer. Be. Bold."

Live life at full throttle. Lead the way. Take risks. Try new things. Inhabit the power with which God has gifted you. Make an impact on your family. Don't let anyone but the Lord set your pace. Don't worry about the haters who call you bossy and controlling. Yes, you have weaknesses like everyone else—we'll look at those in a moment—but don't let anyone or anything keep you from being bold.

Your Top Five Superpowers

While you may not be faster than a speeding bullet or more powerful than a locomotive, the swiftness with which you conquer your grocery shopping and the strength of your ability to handle a child meltdown inspires admiration in the eyes of other moms.

I want to share with you the five top superpowers you possess as a Doer Mom.

Let this list affirm you. Let it declare the beauty of your design. But let it also challenge you as you use the question at the end of each description to take you to a new level in using your strengths to bless your children.

1. You're a motivating mom. Like a pair of jumper cables, you spark your family into motion. You set goals for your children, and the force that is you propels them through each developmental milestone. Whether they're learning how to swim, how to make their own lunches, or how to apologize to friends, you push them to give their best efforts so they can live to their full potential. Some moms believe in letting things happen. Not you. You're the mom who makes things happen.

When Ansley considered jumping from the freshman volleyball team to the JV team, but was unsure if she could do it, I encouraged her to set her mind on the prize and go big. When Casey was considering a new sport, diving, I urged her to try it and drove her clear to another county to find a pool with diving boards. When Caroline was thinking about running for school office, I advised her to go for it and helped her design her campaign poster and classroom speech. When Savannah wanted to get into a top-tier college halfway across the country, I found ways to make the finances work. When Savannah graduates with a chemical engineering degree this year, I'll buy her cap and gown and be her loudest cheerleader when she walks across the stage to receive her diploma. Could my daughters have done these things without my help? Probably. But they will all tell you that mom's boldness to believe in them and spur them on when they were ready to give up helped them live to their full potential.

How has your motivation helped your kids grow into their potential?

2. You're a decisive mom. Unlike other moms who need time to think through their responses, you don't hesitate. You're a mom who knows what you want and what your children need, so you make up your mind quickly. When everyone's wondering whose turn it is on the monkey bars, you have the answer. When Trevor whines, Wyatt hits the dog, or Carmen tells lies, you have immediate solutions. You don't even have to be completely right (this is our little secret, because to you, a bad choice is better than no choice at all). What's important is movement, forward progress, and clear direction.

How have your quick decisions benefitted your family?

3. You're an organized mom. You've got dinner in the crockpot, your to-do list compiled, and a load of laundry folded in the basket before anyone tumbles out of bed, because time is a precious commodity for you. You don't waste time with complicated recipes, decorative knick-knacks, or anything that is too detailed. You're the first one to throw something away or give it to Goodwill if it's no longer useful or practical. You keep things simple and efficient. You don't need your drawers to be perfectly ordered but you do like bins and baskets to keep stuff grouped and out of the way. All your efforts ensure that appointments won't be missed, forms won't be forgotten, and homework is completed by the due date.

In what ways has your organization made life better for your kids?

4. You're a multi-tasking mom. How do you do it all? That's what everyone wants to know. Your secret lies in your ability to manage multiple things at the same time, because your brain can switch quickly between tasks. While the kids take a bath, you clean the sink. While you wait at the doctor's office, you plan meals for the week. (I once did this while waiting for a play to start, and my middle school daughter, who had brought a friend with us, was horrified by my stunning display of time management.) You have a strong work ethic and a strong need to be productive, which enables you to meet the daily demands of motherhood and so much more.

How does your family benefit from your ability to multi-task?

5. You're a brave mom. You've got nerve, girl, and you use it on behalf of your family. You love fiercely. You protect passionately. You fight against the messages of this world that seek to steal the purity of your children, dampen their joy, or destroy their self-worth. You don't shrink back from conflict. You're a lover because you're a fighter. If anyone threatens your children or hurts them intentionally, you go to battle. I once found myself in the middle of my driveway, still in pajamas, yelling at a mom who had unfairly accused my daughter of bullying. Not my finest hour, but I had to stand against the injustice. A lioness lives in you. I pity the fool that comes after one of ours.

How has your courage protected your children?

As a mom, you have opportunities every day to lead and influence your family using your five superpowers. These superpowers greatly influence your leadership style.

Follow the Leader

"I don't feel like a leader now that I'm a stay-at-home mom," said Megan, soon-to-be mom of two. "At my last job, I was in charge of 2,000 volunteers and a staff of twenty-five people. I planned events, provided direction, and saw each project through to completion."

"Would you say you were in full bloom as a leader?" I asked.

"Yes, and it felt great. I felt useful. Now I feel useless, at least compared to what I used to do. I love my son, and I'm grateful that I can stay home with him, but something's missing."

"If you had to put a label on what's missing, what might that be?"

"Purpose," Megan said without hesitation. "I don't feel like I have a strong sense of purpose as a mom."

"What was your purpose when you worked outside the home?"

"I had three primary purposes: I coordinated large events from conception to clean-up. I was responsible for staff development. And it was up to me to make sure that my client's vision was put into action throughout the organization."

"Can't you do the same thing at home?"

Megan laughed. "You mean with a three-year-old and a baby?"

"Megan, your leadership skills are just as important with two as with 2,000."

I gave her a moment to think about that. Then I said, "Would you be willing to work with me to write a mission statement for your role as a leader of your home? And would you like to explore how you can help your own children grow in their skills and abilities so that they can reach their full potential spiritually, emotionally, and physically?"

Megan's eyes lit up. "I'd love to. When can we start?"

It only took a couple coaching sessions for Megan to reframe her view of leadership so it fit her work at home.

You, as a Doer Mom, are a born leader. Let's look at some of the leadership skills you bring to the table.

You're a leader who is in charge. You rise to a position of leadership in most everything you do: president of your moms' group, Girl Scout leader, chair of the eighth-grade continuation committee. You are large and in charge, which is why you love being a mom because you're the boss. Your children respect your authority and appreciate the control you bring to the chaos of life. You provide your family with direction and guidance, whether it's where to find their winter gloves or how to handle problems with friends. You always seem to know what to do, and others love you for that.

You're a confident leader. You believe in yourself and your capabilities. You don't need others to tell you what to do or even to give you maternal advice because you can figure things out on your own. Installing a new car seat? You don't even need the instructions. Dealing with a child who's defiant? You tackle it head-on. Working with the school to get your child the services he or she needs? You'll push through until it happens. You trust your instincts. Your confidence puts your children at ease. They follow you wherever you go.

You're a forthright leader. You're outspoken and direct about saying what's on your mind. You call it like you see it. "That shirt smells like someone died." "You may not speak to another adult in that way." "It's just a scratch, walk it off." Playing the "bad cop" rarely makes you popular, but you know that while the truth may sometimes sting in the moment, you trust that your straightforward approach will help them over time. It's the difference between hurt and harm. Having to hear a hard truth may hurt now, but it will keep them from harm later.[28]

You're a responsible leader. You willingly carrying the weight of your family on your shoulders. You find great satisfaction in fulfilling duties at home, church, school, and work, and you're always ready to take on more. "People with strong responsibility talents take psychological ownership for anything they commit to, whether it is large or small, and they feel emotionally bound to follow it through to completion."[29] When my four girls were young, I felt a responsibility to train them to be responsible future roommates and spouses that would bless those with whom they lived, so I taught them how to do household chores and yardwork. My goal was to model a strong work ethic so I could show them how to carry their own loads. I'm responsible. I want my kids to be responsible, too.

You're a challenging leader. You prompt your children to face their demons, apply themselves, and live to their capacity. You provide the structure and accountability your kids need to reach their goals. Sticker charts for the summer reading contest. Practice times to make the competitive dance squad. Your competitive nature drives your family forward at full speed, growing stronger, and daring greatly. I often told my daughters, "You can do hard things." Those words kept them from stagnating in their comfort zones (parenting that is too soft) or feeling pressured to perform perfectly (parenting that is too hard). Like Goldilocks, I found this instruction to be just right.

It's true! You are amazing with your five distinctive superpowers and your unique style of leadership. But that doesn't ensure that bullets will bounce off your chest! Yes, you are a super mom, but like all of us, you have your vulnerabilities. Let's consider these now.

Doer Mom Kryptonite

All superheroes come with inherent weaknesses. Sad but true. (Unless, of course, you are Wonder Woman, who is an anomaly even in the superhero world.) For instance, Ironman is completely dependent on that little reactor inside his chest to keep him alive. Without it, he's a goner. He also has memory lapses and can't commit. Women, especially, find that to be a problem. And don't forget about his arrogance. It keeps him from playing well with others. And you, Super Doer Mom, with your slice of God's image, have your own vulnerabilities.

As difficult as it may seem, I ask you to embrace these weaknesses. Remember, we all have shortcomings, but I promise that your weaknesses can become your ticket to greater connection with others and greater connection with God. Because it is when we are weak that God makes us strong (2 Corinthians 12:10).

I've put these weaknesses in the form of questions because, more than likely, these are the questions you ask yourself when you're ensnared in a weakness.

Why am I so impatient? When your neighbor tells you a lonnnggg drawn-out story, it drives you nuts because you just want him to cut to the chase. When your kids run late, your frustration mounts with each passing minute. When traffic moves slowly, when people ramble or repeat themselves, when people in charge are all talk and no action, you want to strangle them because they are wasting your time.

Activity that is inefficient or fails to promote forward progress makes you want to crawl out of your skin.

What should you do? "Slow down. Take a deep breath. What's the hurry? Why wear yourself out? Just what are you after anyway?" (Jeremiah 2:25 MSG).

This verse is for all us Doers, so please. Stop. Take a deep breath. All the time. Deep breathing has a calming effect on the nervous system. Relax your shoulders and unclench your jaw. Another thing you can do when someone continues to talk . . . and talk . . . and talk . . . is to say, "I'm sorry to interrupt you, but I have to run." Or set your timer on your phone before you sit down to talk so when it goes off you have an excuse to leave. Unless you are running a race, there are no prizes for getting there first, just like there are no prizes for getting through labor without an epidural.

Why am I so bossy? In an effort to maintain control, you can come across to others as dominant and intimidating. Overbearing. Pushy. My way or the highway. Especially if you're hormonal. Like a drill sergeant with a pack of fresh recruits, you can start to bark orders at your kids when they fall out of line or disobey you. Whether they are toddlers learning the word "no" or teenagers trying to find their own way, you'll use the force of your will to make them comply. The danger here is that your family can fear you more than God.

First Peter 5:2–3 says, "Be shepherds of God's flock that is under your care, watching over them . . . not lording it over those entrusted to you" How do you keep from "lording over" those in your charge? Try relinquishing some control. Not all control, you're the mom after all, but some. Offer them choices that you're comfortable with so they can practice exerting their own wills. For example, let them choose what they wear to school. (This can be embarrassing if your child has too much flair or zero taste. For a whole year, one of my daughters rocked the monochromatic look that she mistakenly believed was hip and trendy.) Give them the responsibility to clean up their toys or make their beds. Let them choose when they do the dishes—right after dinner or before bed.

Why do I hurt others' feelings? Because you value productivity, you tend to prioritize tasks above people. You'll choose cleaning your house over playing with your kids. You'll put more time into completing your errands than hanging out with your family. When your to-do list is long or you're behind schedule, relationships take a backseat. Who has time for sensitivity when you've got to get dinner on the table? Right? When this happens, it's easy for you to miss the emotional cues others give you. You don't mean to, but it happens. You basically run right over them.

Remember, "love is not rude" (1 Corinthians 13:5 NCV).

Ask your children if they feel you care more about what they do instead of who they are. If the answer is yes, ask when or where this happens. Then own it. Apologize and tell them you are sorry. I've been most successful in engaging with my kids when I make them my task. I schedule time with them and mark it on my calendar—dates, outings, a mother-daughter trip. As a Doer, I will always lead with a task orientation, but I want my children to know that they are vitally important to me and, when we are together, I'm all theirs.

Why don't I ask for help? Your gift for autonomy, when taken to the extreme, becomes self-reliant and self-sufficient—qualities guaranteed to produce pride and isolation. For example, on my good days, I love feeling capable and competent as I get stuff done. All. By. Myself. But when my responsibilities become overwhelming (like they have as a single mom), I've had to learn to receive from others.

Just as Moses' father-in-law calls him out in Exodus 18:14 (MSG), "What's going on here? Why are you doing all this, and all by yourself, letting everybody line up before you from morning to night?" Us Doers need to stop doing everything on our own.

There is no shame in needing something. Remember, you are a slice, not the whole pie. You were never designed to be or do everything, so let someone else help when you need it. Do you need a babysitter for the afternoon? A ride for your child? Help with your sprinkler system? I'll admit, it's humbling to ask for help, but it always draws me closer to others and gives me a deep appreciation for their gifts of grace to me.

Why can't I relax? You live in a constant state of motion from the minute your feet hit the floor until your head hits the pillow. You rarely take a soaking bath or go for a "stroll." You hate to sit—it makes you feel guilty. You're all about productivity so when you see others vegging in front of the TV for hours, you think, "How can anyone do that?" Beneath the surface of all your activity lies a murmur of discontent that will eventually wear you and your children out. And if you're not careful, it will force you to relax in the form of injury or illness.

Psalm 23:2 is a verse for Doers. It says, "He makes me lie down in green pastures" (italics mine).

Before God makes you rest, make that choice yourself. Turn on soothing music. Take a walk (not a run) outside. Take a twenty-minute power nap. Fifteen years ago, I started doing hot yoga as a cross-training activity. It's athletic enough for my Doer style, but it taught me how to relax my body. In the beginning, while I'd be working hard holding warrior pose, the teacher would put her hands on my shoulders and ask me to soften them. At first, I didn't understand what she was talking about. But slowly, over time, I learned how to work and relax at the same time.

What's My Trigger?

Every mom has a trigger, a button that, when pushed, can morph her into a "Make My Day" mom.

Irritation simmers inside you. Frustration mounts. If this isn't stopped immediately, you become angry and hostile until it erupts into full-blown rage. This is when your kids take cover.

What's the cause of this mommy meltdown?

Let me tell you straight up.

The thing that triggers you is the **loss of control.**

That's right. Raise your hand if you're a control freak. (My hand was the first one up.)

Look at your triggers. When your children mutiny and won't follow your lead. When they blow off their chores and don't pull their own weight. When your furnace blows up and you have to spend the vacation fund to fix it. When you are forced to wait for someone before moving ahead. All these triggers spring from the frustration you feel over the loss of control.

Control—the power to direct people's behavior or the course of events—means more to you than other personality types because your heart's desire is to make things happen, to overcome obstacles, and solve problems that slow things down. It makes sense. Your sense of urgency and your strong will have been designed for action so you feel diminished when you can't be in charge, or when something gets in the way of your forward momentum.

So how do you prevent your trigger from changing you into scary mommy?

Take note of your level of self-control.

Self-control is the ability to exert command over yourself—your words, your emotions, your actions. When you have self-control, you make deliberate decisions and steward your own life. When you are focused on controlling others, you restrict their abilities to choose and keep them from the gift God gave to them: their own free will.

The more control you exert over yourself, the less pressure you'll feel to exert control over others.

Take a moment right now and ask yourself: Where does my life feel out of control? Is it your marriage? Are there problems you feel powerless to fix? Is it something with your children? Behaviors that you wish were different? Maybe your finances feel out of control? Or a situation in your workplace? Do you, or someone close to you, have health concerns that can't be corrected?

The ultimate answer is to embrace God's control over your life. He has plans for you (Jeremiah 29:11). He directs your steps (Proverbs 20:24 NLT). His purposes for you will prevail (Proverbs 19:21). He won't let you be tempted beyond your ability (1 Corinthians 10:13). He works all things for your good (Romans 8:28). In Him, all things hold together (Colossians 1:17).

While you may feel powerless when you are triggered, be assured that God remains all-powerful at all times and in all ways. He's got this and He's got you, so let Jesus take the wheel.

Let Him know how scared you are to relinquish control. Ask Him to help you trust Him more. Remind yourself of His sovereignty over all things by writing the verses above on your bathroom mirror.

Pray the Serenity Prayer, regularly:

"God grant me the serenity to accept the things I cannot change, the courage to change the things I can, and the wisdom to know the difference."

Trusting God is the first practice that will keep you from being triggered. The second practice is something that doesn't come easy, but is vital for you and your family.

Self-Care Is Not for Sissies

Self-care gets a bad rap by us Doers, because we rarely see the need for it. While bubble baths and deluxe pedicures may sound nice, we secretly believe they're a waste of time. Who wants to lie around all day getting pampered when there's so much that needs to be done?

Right?

As Alan Kraft says in *Good News for Those Trying Harder,* "To those who love to be productive, rest is a lot of work."[30]

Self-care isn't easy for us, but I hope you'll agree that even we need a break. We need to replenish our energy, refresh our minds, and restore our souls.

Here are the most important things that you, as a Doer Mom, can do to take care of yourself.

Set God goals. You mentally set goals related to everything you do. Do the same for your spiritual life. First and foremost, put "time with God" on your to-do list every day. Each morning, when you wake at 5 a.m. (admit it, that's you) and read your devotional, ask God how to live out that truth in the next twenty-four hours. Set a goal—His goal—and go for it. You will never be more productive than when you are sitting with the King of the universe and allowing Him to give you the inside scoop on what really needs to be done. And you will never be more effective than when you are doing that work with Him.

In John 15:5, Jesus says, "apart from me you can do nothing." For years, that verse confused me because, to be honest, I could do a lot of things myself: achieve goals—cooking, cleaning, driving— all before 8 a.m. and not all of them with Jesus. How was that nothing? (I didn't say I was proud of this, only that it's part of my story.) What I've come to understand is that all my doing, if not directed by God, will only have a Doer-sized impact. While that may seem great to me, in the spiritual realm, it is nothing compared to the God-sized effect await-ing work that's infused by Him.

Train for a triathlon. You've got an abundance of energy and a need to achieve, so combine the two and go for the gold. Whether it's a 10K run, a swimming challenge, or a bicycle race, assert yourself physically. It's not just the exercise you need, it's the process of setting and achieving a goal. You're naturally competitive, not just with others, but especially with yourself. So be ambitious; tackle something big.

Years ago, I set a goal to compete in the Rock 'n' Roll marathon (26 miles!) in San Diego. I trained for six months. My youngest was two and my oldest was nine, so I had to get a babysitter for all the long runs. Money was tight, and my calves were tighter, but I'll never forget the incredible sense of accomplishment when I crossed that finish line five hours after the race began. To this day, it's one of my proudest achievements.

Get a job. You need to achieve something each and every day, weekends and holidays included, in order to feel good about yourself. Once most Doer Moms get the hang of motherhood, they get bored because they need goals, accomplishments, and something big to call their own.

Take on a position, paid or unpaid, with some weight. Volunteer for a leadership role at your MOPS group or PTO. Start a book club, a life group, or a home-based business. When my second daughter was a baby, I created my own business, The Spitting Image. I manufactured designer burp cloths for new moms and sold them to boutiques all around the country. I loved the work, the sense of completion that came with each order, and the entrepreneurial spirit. When I became pregnant with my fourth daughter and the demands of the business exceeded the time and energy I had to give, I sold the business and used the money to buy a new minivan.

Celebrate your "all done" list. Before you start your next project or add to your to-do list, it's critical that you stop and celebrate what you've already done. Take a step back and admire your handiwork. Take a photo of your masterpiece and post it on Facebook. Treat yourself to a Starbucks. Make dessert and serve it on the good china. Give God a high-five. Take the family out to dinner. Take the day off.

Celebrating success increases a sense of gratitude. It elevates a feeling of contentment. It provides the closure your soul craves. So before you move on to the next thing, stop and thank God for what was accomplished in the thing you just completed.

Declutter. Research has found that clutter competes for your attention, limiting your ability to focus and process information.[31] Translation: It slows you way down—the worst thing you could ever imagine. So take the time to straighten up your space and organize your schedule. The results will feel better than a massage.

I don't have to tell you how to organize—it's one of your superpowers—but I do want to encourage you to make this a priority. Throw things away. Donate unused items and get them out of your house.

But don't forget to declutter your time, too. When the outside world starts to infringe on your peace with requests, invitations, or pressure to perform, use my favorite phrase: "Thank you, but I'll have to decline." The Latin root of the word decision—cis or cid—literally means "to cut" or "to kill."[32] So use your gift of decisiveness by saying no and eliminating excess in your home and on your schedule.

Remember, not everyone is like you. If your best friend and husband are different personality types, they may not have your same needs for action, achievement, or efficiency. Don't let that deter you. Acknowledge your needs and take care of them. Steward yourself and the superpowers you have to share. Your family will thank you for it.

The next chapter will take this a step further. You'll learn how your design as a Doer Mom mirrors God and what you have been gifted to reflect. You'll also learn how to overcome the lie that you're most likely to believe about yourself and how God wants to inhabit your slice and infuse it with His divinity.

CHAPTER 11

Discover God's Design for Doers

What's your name?

Do you know what it means?

Did you know that your name is a type of inheritance? It's a gift from your parents that speaks of who you are or who you might become. David's name means "beloved," a fitting description for one who became Israel's favorite king. Aaron means "exalted," an apt title for a baby that would one day be the first high priest of Israel.

My name means "valley." Not so great. By definition, a valley or a dale is a low place to be. (I'm sure my parents meant no harm here.) David, Mr. Beloved, wasn't skipping through the dale of hope and good cheer, oh no. In Psalm 23, he's trudging through the valley of the shadow of death. Nice, huh?

But one day, I read a devotional about a valley. This devotional described it as the greenest place on Earth. A place where, because of its low position, all the water and nutrients flow to saturate and nourish the ground. The dale, as it turns out, is the place of the richest growth.

Now that's an inheritance I can embrace!

I wonder what your name says about you in a way that you might never have imagined. I do know this: Your slice of God's image as a Doer is a beautiful inheritance from your loving Father.

It's a visible declaration of His favor toward you. It's His stamp of approval imprinted on who you are and who He made you to be. God likes who you are. He made you this way. When He looks at you, He smiles because you remind Him of Himself. Let me tell you how.

Your Inheritance

Like you, God is a doer. God makes stuff happen. He created the sun, the moon, the stars, and all the creatures on this planet. He parted the Red Sea. He provided manna in the desert. He fought on behalf of His people and led them into the Promised Land. He sent Jesus to show us what He could and would do. Over and over in scripture, we see God doing wonderful things for His people.

Jesus commends doing in John 13:17, "Now that you know these things, you will be blessed if you *do* them" and again in Matthew 7:24, "Everyone who hears these words of mine *and puts them into practice* is like a wise man who built his house on the rock" (italics mine). James exhorts us to be *doers* of the word, and not merely hearers (James 1:22). Doing is a good thing, a God thing.

Like you, God initiates. He goes first. He went looking for Adam and Eve in the Garden when they were actively trying to hide their sin and shame. He made the first move with Moses by contacting him through a burning bush. Christ went first, dying for us while we were still sinners (Romans 5:8). It was He who chose us, not the other way around (John 15:16). God found me in a family that didn't go to church or know anything about Him. I wasn't seeking Him, but He sought me out and made me His own. AND the only way that we are able to love others is because He loved us *first* (1 John 4:19).

Like you, God is a multi-tasker. He hears and answers millions of prayers at the same time. He speaks to His sheep all over the globe at the same time. He acts on behalf of His people every minute of every day simultaneously. He's everywhere, doing it all. Where can we go from His presence? Nowhere. He's already there, getting things done. And He's got all the time in the day and night to do it. Remember, He doesn't ever slumber or sleep. He spends every waking minute working all things together for good all at the same time.

Like you, God is brave. As Oswald Chambers said, "Oh, the bravery of God in trusting us!"[33] Isn't that the truth! That He would put the gospel—His good news for the whole world—into the hands of twelve everyday guys and now us, is a bold move. That Jesus would rebuke Satan in the desert, confront the moneychangers in the temple, and allow Himself to be crucified for the sins of the world shows us His courage.

Like you, God is a warrior. He fights on your behalf. "The Lord will march out like a champion, like a warrior he will stir up his zeal; with a shout he will raise the battle cry and will triumph over his enemies" (Isaiah 42:13).

One of my favorite verses, that now hangs in my family room, is Exodus 14:14, "The Lord will fight for you; you need only to be still." It reminds me that during the most significant battle I had to fight on behalf of my children, God was the one doing the fighting.

Like you, God overcomes obstacles. He overcame the problem of sin through the blood of Jesus (Ephesians 1:7). He triumphed over the dominion of darkness and the sting of death through Christ's great sacrifice. He conquered Satan, and will one day hurl him down and throw him into the lake of burning sulfur. Whatever problem you can imagine, God has the answer. "In this world you will have trouble. But take heart! I have overcome the world" (John 16:33).

Doesn't it make you feel good to read about the many ways that you are like God? Doesn't it make you stand a little taller? Feel a bit more confident? I sure hope it does.

God wants you to know of His loving intention behind your design, but He also needs you to be aware that your slice has an Achilles' heel, an area of weakness, that is vulnerable to a lie. This lie can remain dormant for years, rendering you clueless to its existence. But make no mistake. It is extremely dangerous. So dangerous that, if it's not weeded out, it can lead you astray and away from the One you reflect.

The Lie

My hashtag has always been *#OverAchiever*. Whatever was before me in any phase of life, I worked hard at it. In high school, I filled every waking hour with honors classes, cheer practice, and my part-time job as a busgirl at a French restaurant. In college, I worked extra hard to get into graduate school, joining multiple societies, performing lab tests, and completing my thesis on a tropical sea anemone. (I'm still trying to figure out how to apply that knowledge to my regular life.) When I transitioned into medical sales, I traveled eighty percent of the time and worked around the clock seeing customers during the day and doing paperwork at night.

Once I hung up my briefcase for full-time motherhood, I was on it. 150 percent. All the time. Cleaning, baking, driving, teaching, organizing, training, managing. You know what I mean. You do it all day long. My favorite verses were any that contained the words: *Make every effort ...*

Until I wasn't on it anymore. I was thirty-eight when my efforts took a nose dive. I had four children under the age of eight, which required more energy than my body could produce. My fourth child had come into our world with a host of allergy problems that required a great deal of my time and effort. I applied countless lotions and potions that did little to soothe her pain but left impressive grease stains on the furniture. Another child was diagnosed with ADHD, which required new strategies to manage her special challenges. I had thought that our super organic lifestyle (which required ridiculous amounts of effort) would have shielded us from disorders like ADHD, but clearly, I was wrong (if I'd known that, I might have snuck in Cap'n Crunch more often).

Our finances were tight—that required effort. My marriage was strained—that required effort. And my body was big. After my last pregnancy, no amount of effort could squeeze my body into anything, *and I mean anything!* in my closet. I was in over my head and I couldn't do it anymore.

I started to wonder: *Who was I if I couldn't keep all the balls in the air?*

Who was I if my effort wasn't heroic and my service wasn't significant?

Who was I if the best I could do was to feed my kids, and bathe myself a couple times a week?

Do you see the danger I was in? Do you see what happened to me? Somewhere along the way, I had believed a lie, one that every Doer must address at some point. The lie I believed is this: ***I am more valuable when I am highly productive.***

The problem is that my *identity* had become tangled with my *personality*. I confused my value with my gifting. My worth had become attached to the strengths of my slice rather than my place in the family of God.

Have you ever believed the lie?

On some level, haven't you felt like God was disappointed in you when you couldn't pull it all off? When you had nothing to show for your work or you simply couldn't work anymore? Haven't you felt worthless or useless when you've lost your job, been injured, or stuck on bedrest? Haven't you felt more acceptable and presentable when you could carry all the weight? Haven't you felt more pleasing to God, others, and even yourself when you're giving 150 percent and being productive?

Enough is enough. It's time to pull this lie out from the shadows, wrestle it to the ground, and send it to the pit of hell where it belongs. You are too precious to God to continue living this lie.

Dear Doer, you simply must face your fear that you are nothing without your own efforts. You must put to death right here and now the lie that your work is what makes you visible and valued. No. The truth is this: You are loved, accepted, and seen because you are God's daughter, not because of anything you do, no matter how impressive. Whether you work hard or not, you are of great worth and value.

Yes, God gave you the strengths of the Doer slice—strength, productivity, and courage—but as Job pointed out: "The Lord gave and the Lord has taken away" (Job 1:21).

You can't get around it.

God prunes (John 15:2). He sometimes even cuts away the greatest assets in your life and renders them ineffective and seemingly useless, like He did in my life, but during these times, I believe He's doing the most significant work He'll ever do in your heart. You see, God must remove anything in which you've placed your confidence that is false or flimsy, even if that means rescinding the strengths of your slice. Anything that you love more than God, things that make you feel more acceptable, more presentable, more likable, or more loveable— must be dethroned. It's only when you are completely naked, stripped down to your most raw self, and fully accepted in that state, that you will know that your value rests in His love and not in your strengths.

It hurts, this cutting away. And yet it is so necessary. God goes deep to lay a new foundation. He removes the old structures upon which you've instinctively built your worth and value (whether you knew you were doing that or not), and replaces your lie with an important truth. The truth is this: **Jesus delights in you *not* because you are productive but because you are *His*.**

The Journey to Truth

As a Doer, I had to come to the end of my energetic rope and do the unthinkable:

Stop working. Cease striving. Rest.

It was the hardest thing I've ever done.

During that season, I started attending Celebrate Recovery (CR), a Christian recovery program offered at my church, to address the pain and problems in my life. To be honest, it was a more pierced and tattooed population than I was used to, but they were also the most authentic people I had ever met. From the beginning, I wanted to get involved and help out in leadership, serve as a group facilitator, or even participate as a childcare worker, but they wouldn't let me. They told me to come, sit, and listen. Nothing more.

Easier said than done.

I felt useless. Like I was taking up space.

I felt worthless. Like I was a nobody.

But I also felt convicted.

I realized that because doing and working are woven into a Doer's DNA, my natural inclination was to approach God with a sense of duty and diligence, rather than an attitude of stillness and rest. As a result, I had judged women who appeared idle, weak, or lazy—women who clearly weren't giving God their best effort—and that list now included me. At CR, I learned to embrace the fact that I *was* one of those women. I started to see myself in a whole new light: as a mom who needed to rest as much as I needed to work. As a mom who had intrinsic value without having to earn it. As a mom whose identity was found not in the completion of my spiritual to-do list, but in my completion by Christ (Colossians 2:10 NLT).

It was one of the most transformative seasons of my life: unnerving, terrifying, and extremely challenging. And yet it is one for which I am eternally grateful because, in the midst of that humbling time, I came to understand that my worth was not dependent on my effort. "You're blessed when you're at the end of your rope," we'd say as we repeated the Beatitudes every week. "With less of you there is more of God and his rule" (Matthew 5:3 MSG). While hard to believe at first, I became more comfortable with "less of me" as the members of the group wholeheartedly accepted me in my weakened state and valued me with no performance on my part.

With "more of God," life became balanced and less strenuous. I learned that, while God created me in Christ Jesus for good works, He wasn't giving out points for effort. As Skye Jethani says, "God does not judge our effectiveness. He judges our faithfulness."[34]

One passage of scripture that came to have special meaning to me during that time was Matthew 11:28–30. It spoke of a gentle God who didn't need me to work night and day, but instead wanted to give me rest.

> Come to me, all you who are weary and burdened, and I will give you rest. Take my yoke upon you and learn from me, for I am gentle and humble in heart, and you will find rest for your souls. For my yoke is easy and my burden is light.

God taught me how to yoke to Him—to operate in His strength instead of my own. But He had to start with some clarification. You see, whenever I had seen the word "yoke" in the past, I envisioned a harness: a set of straps placed on an animal so it could get to work. In my mind, I'd be the horse and Jesus would be the driver. But that was wrong. A yoke is actually a frame meant for two. It's a wooden cross-piece shaped to fit over the necks of a pair of animals, so they could pull together. In that scenario, Jesus and I would be working side-by-side. He would be the lead, providing the strength and the direction, and I would be at work alongside Him.

And that is what I did. I'd start each morning by picking up His yoke and letting Him direct my work for the day. Which was interestingly less strenuous than the work I had been trying to pull off on my own. I no longer needed to work like a madman because my effort wasn't attached to my value, so I could move at His pace. If I started to hold my breath, grit my teeth, or tie my shoulders in knots to make things happen, I knew that I had wiggled out of the yoke. I'd confess my independent ways and take His yoke upon me again. What I found in the yoke was what I had always been searching for: rest for my soul.

The answer for Doer women everywhere is to embrace rest—a journey through the desert of human weakness to the heights of divine strength. Regardless of the road you take or are taken on, the destination is still the sweetest spot on Earth: the heart of God.

Your Slice "on God"

If you would like to see what the Lord can do with your strengths, what your slice looks like "on God," you'll want to embrace the same spiritual practice that I did.

Rest.

Rest is a pause. It's a cessation of work. A restraint from labor or exertion. A state of inactivity. Rest is a surrender to God's control and acknowledgment that He is working so you don't have to.

When you rest, you'll find real strength.

When you rest, you'll find true power.

When you rest, you'll find divine peace.

If you're new to rest, let me offer three practical tips that may help you establish this daily practice:

1. Take a Sabbath. In the Old Testament, God was so adamant that His children rest that He included the idea in His Top Ten Commandments. He established one day out of seven in which the Israelites were to cease all work and take a Sabbath, a day of rest to focus upon God. "Remember the Sabbath day by keeping it holy. Six days you shall labor and do all your work, but the seventh day is a Sabbath to the Lord your God" (Exodus 20:8–10).

Jesus, Himself, kept the Sabbath, and encourages us to do the same.

This is a time management issue for which you are well-equipped. Organize your family, your home, and yourself, for a day of rest. Attend to important work on Saturday, so that by Sunday, you unplug and unwind. Do your chores and shopping during the week. Turn off your television, your computer, and, at the very least, mute your phone. Ignore the bills, the dust, the clutter—just for the day. Do nothing in which you feel productive. Whatever work you don't finish ahead of time remains—piles of laundry, scattered toys, dirty dishes. It's okay. Simply walk around them, knowing that every time you do, your Sabbath inaction is further dismantling the lie of your slice.

And then, enjoy the purpose of the Sabbath. Enjoy time to read the Bible. Enjoy an extra-long time of prayer. Enjoy God's creation. Enjoy a walk or a nap. Enjoy silence or the praise of worship music. Enjoy your kids by playing with them on the floor or in the yard.

Enjoy a bike ride, a good book, or anything that provides a deep feeling of rest.

2. Ask for help. As an independent, you usually don't involve others because they slow you down. But God *wants* you to slow down and to involve Him in everything you do. It only takes a few moments to pause and ask Him to help you with the task at hand. The blowout diaper. The meal for the Johnsons. The mystery of your son's behavior.

Let God carry the weight of your family. Let Him do the heavy lifting. You're strong but He is stronger. Give your heart and mind a rest by yoking with God at all times and in all ways, asking for His wisdom, His strength, and His power.

One of my favorite plaques, that sat on the ledge above my bedroom door where I would see it when I first woke up, read, "Good morning. This is God. I will be handling all your problems today." It allowed me to start each and every day with a sense of rest and relief.

3. Abide. In John 15:4 Jesus teaches us that the secret to real fruitfulness, aka divine productivity, is found in abiding. "Remain in me, as I also remain in you. No branch can bear fruit by itself; it must remain in the vine. Neither can you bear fruit unless you remain in me." If we are to reach our full potential as a fruit-bearer, we must learn to abide in the vine (Jesus). Eternal fruit (productivity) doesn't happen on its own. It happens through abiding.

In his classic book on the Gospels, J. C. Ryle says,

> To abide in Christ means to keep up a habit of constant close communion with Him—to be always leaning on Him, resting in Him, pouring out our hearts to Him, and using Him as our fountain of life and strength, as our chief companion and best friend.[35]

To abide in Christ is to make every minute of our day close and personal with God. Brother Lawrence describes it as "conversing with God continually and referring to Him in all I do."

Abiding is noticing God with you in the laundry room, listening to God while you are in the car, and obeying God in every situation in which you find yourself. Oswald Chambers says, "There is no condition in life in which we cannot abide in Jesus."[36] Granted, he wasn't a mom, but if anyone can abide amidst the clutter and the chaos, it is a Doer.

I'll leave you with this excerpt from *The Kitchen Prayer* by Klara Munkres. These words can help you abide in this season of life.

O Lord of pots and pans and things,
Since I have no time to be
a great saint by doing lovely things,
or watching late with Thee,
or dreaming in the dawnlight,
or storming Heaven's gates,
Make me a saint by getting meals,
and washing up the plates.
Warm all the kitchen with Thy Love,
and light it with Thy peace;
Forgive me all my worrying,
and make my grumbling cease.
Thou who didst love to give men food
in room, or by the sea,
Accept the service that I do-
I do it unto Thee.[37]

Now, let your Father tell you how He feels about you and the beauty of your slice.

My **Doer** Daughter,

From the moment you were conceived, I infused into your frame an intuitive knowledge that the world you entered is passing away and you have only a short time to impact others with your actions and energy. This explains the restless urgency you feel that others do not and why efficiency drives everything you do. Along with this knowledge, I knit into your soul visible gifts of leadership, organization, and authority. You have the capacity to handle many things at the same time. I made you both determined and decisive.

Because of your strengths, you are able to accomplish much for Me and to reflect well this aspect of My nature. You desire to work diligently and to achieve. It is important for you to accomplish something meaningful each day to feel good about your contribution. You are a woman of action just as I am a God of action. As My Son said, "My Father is always working and so am I." I am pleased that you, My daughter, can be My hands and feet to make My activity visible in the world by moving good ideas into divine action.

I designed you to be a leader, to motivate others with your energy. Others sometimes see you as controlling because too often you mistake your role for My role. Remember, you are not in control. I am the Sovereign One, the Blessed Controller of all creation. Your job is to partner with Me. Only then will you be most productive and effective in things that really matter.

I know the plans I have for you, plans to use you to mobilize My people, to motivate them, and to move them to action, but you will do the gravest disservice if you allow others to look to you to meet their needs rather than pointing them to Me. Yes, you are strong but you have limits. I have no limits. Remember, I who called you am faithful, and I will also work in you and through you to accomplish My will. Not by your might or power will things be accomplished, but by My Spirit.

Separate from your "to-do" list and be alone with Me. I will become your rest and you will accomplish far more because you abide in My rest.

Remember always that I love you for who you are to Me, not for what you do for Me. I am the creator of power and productivity. I impart these to you as a gift, not as an identity. As you rest in Me, I will flow My power and productivity through you.

I love you, my strong daughter. Look always to Me, your True Mirror, the One who sees you perfectly and completely.

With All My Love,
Your Father

CHAPTER **12**

Slices Unite!

"The body is not made up of one part but of many."
1 Corinthians 12:14

"Mom, I just love the Bulows. They are like the family I never had."

This gut-wrenching comment came from my daughter, Caroline, who had just spent the last five minutes as we drove down Rock Creek Parkway telling me how much she loved her weekend with the Bulow family, how kind and gentle they were, how not like our family they were.

Deep breath, I told myself.

I tried not to react.

I tried not to drive off the road.

I tried not to end her life in that very moment.

The family you never had? Are you kidding me? What in the world have I been doing for the last twenty years? I gave up my career to be at home full time so I could craft a family identity where everyone felt deeply known and fully loved. I taught you biblical principles and Christian val-ues. I planned family-bonding vacations and Hallmark memory moments. Every night at the dinner table, I solicited everyone's crazy highs and lows of the day. The family you never had? Child, did you see any of that?

To my credit, I bit my tongue and said nothing, but internally, my heart broke.

I knew Caroline was referring to the past year. A very rough year for all of us.

You see, when my marriage fell apart, everything changed for the girls and me.

In the first few months, I experienced extreme anxiety. I'd wake up every night at 3:30 a.m. with my mind racing and couldn't get back to sleep. I couldn't stop crying; I couldn't think straight. And for the first time in a long time, I couldn't eat. The upside is that I finally lost those last ten pounds of baby weight that I'd been trying to lose for years.

After I reached out to my doctor for help, I got busy. In addition to my regular mom duties of cooking, cleaning, driving, and counsel-ing (remember, I had four girls who loved to talk), I had to get a job. Speaking at local mom's groups for potpourri and Starbucks cards did not pay the bills, so I chose a new career as a professional life coach. I got my certification and started my own business. I figured out how to manage my finances. I refinanced the house, got my own medical and life insurance, and paid off my car. I took my girls on college tours, helped them apply, and figured out how to pay for it all. I learned how to do my own taxes, repair my sump pump, and re-grout the shower.

I learned to be both mom and dad in every way.

But I still wasn't enough for my girls.

This family that Caroline loved so much brought other aspects of God's love into her life. They were soft and caring, quietly nurturing and faithful. They were humble, gentle, and pleasantly social. (Who has time to be social when your shower needs re-grouting?)

My Doer superpowers of motivating, multi-tasking, and problem-solving may have gotten us through a very tough time, but those qualities could not meet all of my daughter's needs.

Simply put, at this moment, the Bulows could provide things my daughter needed that I could not.

Caroline's words stung. They shamed me. They reminded me that I was not enough.

Have you ever felt like you were not enough?

Most moms I know—no matter what type they are—and even those not in the midst of a life crisis, are haunted by a sense that they are not enough.

In coaching, we call this a limiting belief. It's a way of thinking that holds you back from your true potential and your inherent value. It's a lie that Satan whispers in your ear because he wants you to believe that you are supposed to be everything to everyone. He wants you to judge yourself and belittle yourself and then try to spread yourself so thin that the authentic you is no longer recognizable anymore.

One of the main reasons we feel like we are not enough is because we have an idealized picture of what a good mom should look like.

Here's mine:

A good mom is loving and fun—hers is the house where every child wants to come and play. A good mom is in control. Her kids respect her. A good mom makes all her meals from scratch. A good mom plans and schedules all the date nights with her husband and is low maintenance enough not to burden him with trivial stuff. A good mom is a great decorator. A good mom contributes to the family income but not so much that she compromises her mothering. A good mom reads books and listens to informative podcasts. A good mom leads Bible study and prays not only for her family, but her church leaders, her community, and her nation. A good mom enforces limits on screen time, but it's no biggie because she's so busy engaging her children's minds with quality learning activities, they don't even miss it. A good mom is thin and fit. A good mom has a dog, maybe two. A good mom never criticizes, is always cheerful, and knows her purpose.

A good mom, according to a definition like this, is all things to all people. She doesn't just have a set of skills; she has all of them. She's not just a slice of God's image; she's the whole pie.

The problem is that the "good mom" isn't real. She's artificial. She's a man-made (or woman-made) creation, not the authentic mom God made her to be.

No mom is the whole pie.

All those times I had wished that I was an amazing hostess and master of ceremonies, *and* a superhuman caregiver and diplomat, *and* a talented artist and creative thinker—God knew that what my family needed most would be found in the slice of the Doer. And He would provide the rest.

Variety Pack

Nothing gets more applause in my house than when I come home from the grocery store with fun food. Do you get this too? I dutifully push the organic produce and wholesome ingredients, but snacks bring my kids cheer. And if those snacks—the chips, drinks, or granola bars—happen to come in a variety pack with a big selection of flavors, then I have scored a home run.

Kids love an assortment, and so does God.

He has created the most wonderful assortment the world has ever seen: the body of Christ. The body of Christ is God's family. This clan, our clan, includes all His children, every person who has decided to follow Christ as Lord. The body of Christ is filled with many different types of people and personalities, each with a specific contribution to make.

"Just as each of us has one body with many members, and these members do not have all the same function, so in Christ we, though many, form one body, and each member belongs to all the others. We have different gifts, according to the grace given to each of us" (Romans 12:4–6).

You and your slice were created to be a part of this larger community. You were never made to be everything to everyone, not even your kids.

Say this with me: "I'm not supposed to be all things to all people."

You were put in a variety pack for that. You were made to be just as God intended. As Paul reminds us in 1 Corinthians 12:18, "But in fact God has placed the parts in the body, every one of them, just as he wanted them to be." He wants you to offer your distinctive gifts and talents, and rely on the other slices to offer theirs.

Your variety pack might include your husband, your best friend, or your friends from church. It might include your neighbors, your parents, or your siblings. Maybe, like me, your variety pack includes your children's teachers, coaches, and caregivers. Your assortment is likely to be a mix of the above.

Mother Teresa said, "You can do things that I cannot. I can do things that you cannot. But together we can do great things."[38]

It's the combination of our individual strengths and talents working together that will achieve great things for God.

I was taught and had always believed that "it takes a village" is a cop-out for lazy, irresponsible people. The most honorable thing parents can do, I thought, was to carry their own loads all by themselves.

As it turns out, that is simply not true.

And thank goodness, because as a single mom, it is taking a village of many slices to raise my children.

And while it isn't easy for an independent gal like me to depend upon the slices of others, being in THE variety pack (God's variety pack) has offered me a certain freedom that I didn't expect. Let me share ways trusting in the whole pie has actually made me a better mom.

I am free to be me. I don't have to be ashamed of my limitations or hide who I am. I can be grateful for the superpowers that God has given me and appreciate the superpowers He's gifted to others. I don't have to become someone I'm not in order to be a good mom. I just have to allow God to infuse my strengths with His power and ask Him to fill in my gaps with His people.

I am free to be sharp. Well-roundedness is an illusion. And—forgive the pun—this is the point. As Marcus Buckingham and Donald Clifton, creators of the StrengthsFinder Profile, said in their book *Now Discover Your Strengths:*

> That excellent performers must be well rounded is one of the most pervasive myths we hope to dispel in this book. When we studied them, excellent performers were rarely well rounded. On the contrary, they were sharp.[39]

I no longer have to spend all my time trying to fix my weaknesses. It's okay to have shortcomings. It's not a sin to be average and ordinary in some areas and outright dreadful in others. Granted, I need to manage my weaknesses with God's help, but I now focus more of my time on building my strengths and offering them to others.

I am free from jealousy. Once I understood that God didn't expect me to be the whole pie, I found it much easier to admit my deficits and acknowledge those moms who are "faithful stewards of God's grace in its various forms" (1 Peter 4:10). I didn't have to envy their talents; I could appreciate them. I could enjoy them. My children and I could benefit from them.

What about you? Do you sometimes feel that you are not enough for your family? Do you feel free to be who God made you to be? Are you free to be sharp? Free from jealousy?

As Caroline and I pulled into the driveway that day after her comment about the Bulows, she looked over at me from the passenger seat and said, "Do you know the one thing that my friends are jealous about that I have?"

"What's that?" I asked, thinking "*This had better be good.*"

"They are jealous of my relationship with you."

I smiled. Tears blurred my eyes.

I am not everything, Lord, but I am a slice of Your image. And that is enough because You are enough for us all.

Endnotes

1. E. E. Cummings, *E. E. Cummings: a Miscellany Revised* (University of Michigan: October House, 1965), 13.
2. Ralph Waldo Emerson, *The Complete Works* (New York and Boston: Houghton, Mifflin, 1904), Bartleby.com, 2013.
3. Caroline Leaf, *The Perfect You* (Grand Rapids, MI: Baker Publishing Group, 2017), 33.
4. David G. Benner, *The Gift of Being Yourself* (Downers Grove, IL: InterVarsity Press, 2015), 17.
5. Richard Rohr, *Immortal Diamond: The Search for Our True Self* (San Francisco, CA: Jossey-Bass, 2013), 119–122.
6. Lorraine Pintus, *Jump Off the Hormone Swing* (Chicago: Moody, 2011), 164.
7. William Marston, *Emotions of Normal People* (London: K. Paul Trench, Trubner & Co. Ltd, 1928) and Larry Price, Ph.D., DISC Personality System Validation Study, Texas State University, 2015.
8. Susan Cain, *Quiet: The Power of Introverts In a World That Can't Stop Talking* (New York: Crown Publishers, 2012), 4.
9. Wikipedia contributors, "Masking (personality)," *Wikipedia, The Free Encyclopedia,* https://en.wikipedia.org/w/index.php?title=Masking_(personality)&oldid=818251415, retrieved February 14, 2018.
10. https://www.goodreads.com/quotes/104615-may-today-there-be-peace-within-may-you-trust-god, retrieved October 17, 2018.
11. Edmund Burke, as quoted on www.goodreads.com.
12. Paul Coughlin and Jennifer D. Degler, *No More Christian Nice Girl*

(Bloomington, MN: Bethany House, 2010), 18.

13. L. B. Cowman, Streams in the Desert (Grand Rapids, MI: Zondervan, 1997), 401.

14. Hebrews 4:12, Matthew 10:19–20, Jeremiah 33:3, John 8:47, John 10:27, John 16:13.

15. Ruth Haley Barton, *Invitation to Solitude and Silence: Experiencing God's Transforming Presence* (Downers Gove, IL: Intervarsity Press, 2010), 133.

16. Ann Voskamp, *One Thousand Gifts* (Grand Rapids, MI: Zondervan, 2010), 109.

17. Andy Stanley, *Visioneering* (Colorado Springs, CO: Multnomah, 2016), 179.

18. https://www.quotes.net/quote/12558, retrieved October 24, 2018.

19. Brene Brown, *Daring Greatly* (New York, NY: Penguin, 2012), 42.

20. https://www.psychologytoday.com/blog/high-octane-women/201208/the-mind-and-body-benefits-optimism-0.

21. Daniel Nettle, *Personality* (Oxford, NY: Oxford University Press, 2007), 112–113.

22. Tim Keller, *The Meaning of Marriage: Facing the Complexities of Commitment with the Wisdom of God* (New York, NY: Dutton Adult, 2011).

23. Julia Cameron, *The Artist's Way* (London: Pan Books, 1993), 2.

24. https://www.seeker.com/two-thirds-marine-species-remain-unknown-1766300637.html, DNews, 12/13/12.

25. https://www.space.com/26078-how-many-stars-are-there.html.

26. Shauna Niequist, *Present over Perfect* (Grand Rapids, MI: Zondervan, 2016), 129.

27. Dr. Henry Cloud and Dr. John Townsend, *Safe People* (Grand Rapids, MI: Zondervan, 1995), summarized from 23.

28. Dr. Henry Cloud, *Necessary Endings* (New York, NY: HarperCollins, 2010), 21.

29. Quoted from Responsibility Strengths sheet, Gallup, StrengthsFinder, 2012.

30. Alan Kraft, *Good News for Those Trying Harder* (Colorado Springs, CO: David C Cook, 2008), 109.

31. J. Neurosci. 2011 Jan 12;31(2):587-97. doi: 10.1523/JNEUROSCI.3766-10.2011.

32. Greg McKeown, *Essentialism* (New York, NY: Penguin Random House, 2014), 159.

33. Oswald Chambers, *My Utmost For His Highest* (Uhrichsville, OH: Barbour Books), 217.

34. Skye Jethani, *Immeasurable: Reflections on the Soul of Ministry in the Age of Church, Inc.* (Chicago, IL: Moody, 2017), 26.

35. J. C. Ryle, *Expository Thoughts on the Gospels: St. John, Volume 3* (Robert Carter & Bros, 1880), 104.

36. Oswald Chambers, *My Utmost for His Highest* (Uhrichsville, OH: Barbour Books), 119.

37. Klara Munkres, *The Kitchen Prayer*, (unknown).

38. Mother Teresa, as quoted on www.goodreads.com

39. Marcus Buckingham and Donald Clifton, *Now Discover Your Strengths* (New York, NY: The Free Press, 2001) 128.

Acknowledgments

This book would NEVER have been possible without the heroic commitment and sacrificial effort of Lorraine Pintus, my extraordinary Doer/Improver writing coach. Lorraine opened her home and her heart to me and taught me to first worship, then wait, then write. I am only a writer because of her investment in me.

I would also like to thank Linda Dillow, who infused new life into this project with her divine wisdom and sparkly Connector/Doer personality. And Terry Behimer, my editor, whose discerning eye and Improver mind have simply made this book better. Ken Apodaca, Brooke Neville, and Rachel Rogers each provided invaluable tech support and without their help, there would be no website.

I'm exceedingly grateful to all my coaching clients who have entrusted me with their authentic selves and shown me the beauty of their individual slices. And to Jeff, whose gracious love has helped me see myself as God does. And to my parents, John and Barbara, whose unwavering support has allowed me to do hard things.

And finally to Jesus, who "himself bore my sins in His body on the cross, so that I might die to sins and live for righteousness; by his wounds I have been healed" (1 Peter 2:24, my paraphrase).

About the Author

Dale Wilsher lives in the suburbs of Boulder, Colorado, with her four daughters (Savannah, Casey, Caroline, and Ansley) and down the street from her soon-to-be husband, Jeff.

Dale has been a professional life and strength coach (CPLC, ACC) since 2014. Working with Christian women all over the country, Dale has helped them understand their authentic designs so they can serve with greater impact and live life to the fullest.

As a speaker and trainer, Dale has given hundreds of presentations on the topics of authentic faith, DISC personality types, and intentional parenting. Known for her ability to blend humor and spiritual depth into a real and relevant message, she has inspired thousands of women, teams, and parents toward divine self-awareness and a deeper understanding of others.

Though you'd never take her for a former science geek, Dale has a bachelor's degree in Invertebrate Zoology from the University of Georgia and worked as a microbiologist in graduate school. She took her scientific background and used it to become a dynamic producer in the world of medical sales before hanging up her briefcase for full-time motherhood. These days you can find her running with her best friend, Karin, sweating in hot yoga, or rejoicing over the fact that she no longer runs an Airbnb out of her basement.

If you're interested in having Dale speak to your group, contact her at Hello@YourAuthenticPersonality.com.

Made in the USA
Monee, IL
24 November 2019

17374088R00106